Crowned

Created for Glory,
Called by His Name

A Discipleship Series
By Melissa Deming

Crowned: Created for Glory, Called by His Name

© 2015 by Melissa Deming

Editing by Amanda Williams and Diane King.

To my sisters in Christ
Living Faith Community Church, Pittsburgh

CONTENTS

Introduction	1
Chapter 1: Crowned	7
Chapter 2: Dethroned	23
Chapter 3: Royal Robes	41
Chapter 4: Daughters of the King	63
Chapter 5: Heirs of Grace	81
About the Author	99
About the Artist	101

INTRODUCTION

When my husband and I moved our family across the country from Texas to Pittsburgh, we set out to find the biggest church in our area and hide on the back pew.

But before you choose to close this book because I sound like the last person you'd seek out for spiritual advice, you'll be happy to know that God intervened in our life…in a big way.

A few months after arriving in our new hometown, we found ourselves happily joining the smallest church in the city. Literally. On our first Sunday at Living Faith Community Church, we had the option of sitting in one of twenty available folding chairs. Hiding wasn't going to be an option. In fact, the Southern Baptist church plant had yet to officially open its doors to the public.

On the first Sunday we attended, our GPS led us to the back of an empty electrical workers union office building. As we sat waiting for someone to show up, I became increasingly skeptical how this church could engage, much less contain, my rambunctious three-year-old twin boys who had managed to Houdini themselves out of their car seats. Breaking the silence of disappointment, my husband looked at me and said, "We'll give them another five minutes, and if no one shows up we're going to get pancakes."

We held our breath. I prayed for pancakes. So did the

boys.

But in a way that only God can orchestrate, there were no pancakes to be eaten that morning. Instead, we left Sunday services well-fed on God's Word and authentic New Testament community. On the way home, my pancake-loving husband broke the news. After one hour with these people, he said he felt God calling us to team up with this small cluster of families to see God move in our new city in big ways.

In October 2012, Living Faith Community Church officially launched. Since then, we've seen slow, but steady growth. The largest demographics coming to our church are families and single women, from choice or divorce. As we began to minister to these women and their families, we discovered that many of them could be categorized as "unchurched" – having little or no biblical background. Having been raised in a Southern Baptist church, the spiritual landscape in which I found myself was a different terrain from the cultural underpinnings of the Bible belt. Pittsburgh is a city of 2.5 million people, yet only 7.6 percent are affiliated with any evangelical church, the North American Mission Board estimates.

When these women decide to follow Christ, their spiritual journey often begins from scratch. They are learning things as an adult that I grew up knowing, like the books of the Bible, how to locate chapters and verses, and the divisions of the Scriptures (Old and New Testaments). The discipleship challenges of training women with no Christian worldview was eye-opening for me, despite having discipled women in Southeast Asia a few years prior. Many of the challenges I faced overseas were now mirrored stateside.

The mission field surrounding our church is truly pioneer territory for gospel activity, which makes it exciting and exhausting all at the same time. And as is the case in numerous U.S. cities, the mission field is no longer across oceans, it's across the street, even in the folding chairs and pews of our own churches.

Last summer, the need for discipling these women became so great that I began to piece together a discipleship strategy tailored to women who have no Christian background or prior Bible knowledge. The strategy is also tailored for church plants, to do the specific work among women that must occur in a new church.

In order to see our church's vision fulfilled of being a church planting center in the city, church leadership knew our discipleship strategy must encompass more than growing a woman's knowledge of the Bible. We knew that we needed to produce disciples who could in turn make other disciples. To become a church-planting church, we needed to make disciples who are disciple-makers.

This book comprises just one small aspect of our women's discipleship strategy. It is an initial component, rooting a woman in her identity in Christ with five foundational truths of salvation: creation, redemption, justification, adoption, and sanctification. Keeping our ministry context and purpose in mind, the language is simple enough for an unchurched woman to grasp and simple enough to be reproduced in conversations over coffee.

Each chapter answers two key questions: *Who is God?* and *Who am I in Christ?*

In chapter 1, we learn that God is our good Creator and King who shares his glory with us by crowning us with his very image. In this chapter, we look at the foundational truth of the image of God and what it means for who we are and why we exist.

In chapter 2, we discover that God is our Savior who rescues us from sin through his Son when we rebelled against his throne. We uncover the tragic cause and effect of sin in our lives, relationships, and the world.

In chapter 3, we grapple with God who rules as a

righteous Judge, pardoning our sin and then wrapping us in the royal robes of his Son. We discuss the biblical doctrine of justification, or "being declared right" once again.

In chapter 4, we hear about God's unfathomable love for us as our forever Father and our inheritance as daughters of the King. We learn about the implications of our adoption for everyday living.

And in chapter 5, we uncover the blessings given to us from our holy King as he claims us and cleanses us, making us suitable to share in his glory and serve as heirs of grace with the King of Kings, Jesus Christ. We look at the topic of sanctification and how God restores his image in us by making us look like his Son.

From each of these truths concerning the character and activity of God, we learn the core of our own personal identity: who we are and what we are meant to do. We are, as the title suggests, *Crowned: Created for Glory, Called by His Name.*

Although written with a new believer in mind, ideally, a more seasoned Christian woman would use this book as a teaching guide, walking through the material with a new disciple. We are, after all, equipping disciple-makers, women who can replicate themselves by discipling other women. Moreover, *Crowned* is specifically designed as a discipleship toolbox for a small group or women's ministry. Along with discipleship material embedded into each chapter, the book also contains discussion and study material (called Kingdom Keys) for women seeking deeper study or for leaders to use in preparing their hearts as they disciple others.

One of the most crucial components of this book is its emphasis on Scripture. Ephesians 2:1-10 is a central passage to this study. For a new believer, memorizing 10 verses might seem daunting. Feel free to tailor your group's memorization assignments, memorizing just a few verses with each chapter or simply memorize one verse (such as Eph. 2:10).

This study represents the first of three discipleship classes designed to introduce new and potential believers to foundational truths of Scripture – who they are (worldview), what they believe (biblical literacy), and what they are called to do (missional living). So, I would be terribly remiss if I failed to express my gratitude to the ladies of Living Faith Community Church, Pittsburgh, who laughed and loved me through this study.

I hope this book transforms the way you view God in the Scriptures and, subsequently, how you view yourself and the world. Discipleship must always begin with the King, knowing him and leading others to know him and serve him. As women crowned by him, there is much to do as representatives of his eternal throne.

All the King's love,
Melissa

"The LORD sits enthroned over the flood;
The LORD is enthroned as King forever.
The LORD gives strength to his people;
the LORD blesses his people with peace." Ps. 29:10-11 (NIV)

CHAPTER 1: CROWNED

A couple of years ago, a visitor to the New York Metropolitan Museum of Art fell onto a Pablo Picasso painting from his very rare Rose Period. The woman dented and tore the six-foot canvas.[1] At the time of the accident, the painting, called "The Actor," was said to be valued at over $130 million.

Now, the article doesn't say anything about children being present at the time of the accident, but based on my own personal experience, I'd like to believe that if this poor woman happened to have children in tow, then there is a very good chance they had something to do with it. I have six-year-old identical twins boys. I know how museum visits go. So, let's give this poor woman the benefit of the doubt.

But regardless of how the accident happened, what do you think happened next? Do you think the museum curators simply chucked the painting? Did they say, "Well, that stinks. But we've got a few other Picassos in the back."

No way. Immediately after the accident, museum curators whisked the painting away and began forming a plan of restoration. Museum representatives later called this particular process of restoring the damaged Picasso painting "painstaking." In fact, one restorer said, "It made eye surgery look easy. It is tedious, but there's only one of these paintings, so the effort is worth it."[2]

Something priceless was broken. Throwing it away wasn't an option because there was only one. It had to be restored.

Now, I want to fast forward in the art world to last year when another woman was made famous for her part in restoring a priceless work of art. You've probably heard of her because news of her activity went viral.

A Roman Catholic church in northeastern Spain reported a case of suspected vandalism of a century old "ecce homo" fresco of Jesus, wearing a crown of thorns. Ecce homo means "behold the man" and refers to an artistic motif depicting the Christ Jesus prior to his crucifixion.

The New York Times reported that an elderly woman named Cecilia Giménez finally claimed responsibility for the suspected vandalism revealing that she had tried to restore the fresco, which was painted directly on the church's walls.

Calling it the "the worst art restoration project of all time," the New York Times said Ms. Giménez worked off a 10-year old picture of the painting, but "eventually left Jesus with a half-beard and, some say, a monkeylike appearance."[3]

I share the stories of these two women – the lady who ruined the Picasso painting in New York and Senora Giménez who ruined a century-old mural in Madrid – because they could very well be our stories. In fact, in a spiritual sense they *are* our stories.

Paul tells us in the book of Ephesians that we are

masterpieces. In Eph. 2:8-10, he says, "[8]For by grace you have been saved through faith. And this is not your own doing; it is the gift of God, [9] not a result of works, so that no one may boast. [10] For we are his <u>workmanship</u>, created in Christ Jesus for good works, which God prepared beforehand, that we should walk in them" (emphasis mine).

We are God's "workmanship" or handiwork. In the original language, the word "workmanship" or "handiwork" provides the root for the word "poem," conveying the idea that we are perfectly designed and painted by the Master Artist. We are his masterpiece. We do not exist, as our culture tells us, due to the fortuitous accident of gases and cells colliding together in space. We were created by the purposeful hand of a skilled Artist. And this Artist created us for a very important purpose, based on neither boredom nor whim. The Artist designed us in his very own image, crowning us above all his other breathtaking creations (Gen. 1:26).

Now, here is where our story aligns with Ms. Giménez's story. Despite having a rich history, we fall into sin and do irreparable damage to ourselves. Instead of throwing us in the garbage or painting over us and beginning a completely new painting, God chooses to enter into a painstaking process to restore us back to our original grandeur. But because we are the creation (not the Creator), we are unable to repair the damage ourselves. Only the Artist who stands separate and outside of his art has the ability and skill required to conduct a repair.

Many of us spend our entire lifetimes trying to fix the broken and frayed parts of our lives. We spend all our strength and resources trying to cover up the bare spots in our relationships and marriages with all manner of cultural bandages – retail therapy, self-medication, hook-ups, career advancement, online activity, and more. And the result is that we make an even bigger mess of our lives. We move ourselves farther from God's original creative vision for our lives. Paul tells us in the first few chapters of Ephesians that we cannot fix ourselves (Eph. 1-2:10)We are too broken.

But when we let the Master Artist restore us – when we let him heal the stories of our lives and give us his crown to wear once again – we are even more beautiful than before. In his skillful hand, God is able to use those scars from life's rips and tears to showcase his glory, pointing others to the skillful hand of our Restorer We are finally able to fulfill the grand purpose for which we have been placed on planet earth: to be called by his name and created for glory. We are crowned by him.

GOD IS THE GOOD CREATOR

In each chapter, we will answer two questions: Who is God? And who am I? Two questions to which Scripture alone gives resounding, resolute, and right answers. In this chapter, we are going to unpack the following two truths: God is the Creator, and I am God's good creation.

When we open the first pages of the Bible, we are greeted by a God who created everything out of nothing. And while many cultures share similar stories to account for their beginnings, the biblical story of creation stands distinct. Unlike the way gods of ancient mythology or folklore are portrayed, the God of the Bible is worthy of worship because he is both a good Creator and a good King – one who willingly and joyfully involves himself in the affairs of his kingdom, bringing justice and peace to its inhabitants (Ps. 29:10-11).

These truths ring true from the first page in the Bible. If we were to read the first chapter of the Bible (Genesis 1), we would discover that after God creates something, he declares it "good." Over and over again that is how God describes his artistry. The light? It's good. The water? It's good. The trees? They're good. Animals? They're good. Mankind, very good!

God declares his artistry "good" seven times. So, here's a free little tidbit. Whenever you see the biblical author repeat something in the text, you can bet he has a purpose in repeating himself. In the Scriptures, repetition is not a sign of poor writing skills, but rather a literary device used to emphasize a central truth. So, when the author repeatedly says something is "good," he is communicating that God's creation is good, but more notably, what God *does* is good.

God didn't just create something to admire his handiwork. In Gen. 1, he's not just looking at his work and patting himself on the back. *"Wow, I really did a great job on that. That looks really good. Good job, You!"* In repeatedly calling creation "good," the author of Genesis is highlighting that God's creation is good because it has a very good purpose – it mirrors his goodness.

When God created the first kingdom, he wasn't just creating people, places, and things. He was designing and establishing a good pattern of life for it – a peaceful type of life. It looked like man and woman living in harmony with their holy King, with each other, and with the whole created order.

I had just wrapped up a speaking event at a conference in Colorado, outlining the King's kingdom as the central theme of all the Scriptures, when a college student approached me with a question.

"Where do you get that God is the King?" the young lady asked. "I don't see that anywhere in Genesis."

The college student rightly understood that Genesis revealed God to be the Creator, but she was having trouble seeing the connection to a royal throne. Here's her question in a nutshell: why does the Creator of the world also get to be the King of the world?

I explained to her that the book of Genesis is the opening act of God's story; the act of creation is the first major plot move in the Bible. Without this first plot move, there would be no remaining parts of the biblical story. Save for the Creator, we would have no personal stories at all.

Herein lies the connection between God's role as Creator and his title as King. Because God is the Creator, he has the natural right to rule over his creation. In the same way that recording artists squabble over full ownership rights of their music, the work of God's hands belong solely to him. All creation belongs to him, to reap the benefits and glory that come from it. God, then, is more than the Creator of the earth; he is its Ruler Supreme. He is the King of the cosmos.

As our world increasingly denies God to be the Creator of the world, it also, unwittingly or purposefully, dethrones God as its one true King. This is the quandary of the modern woman, for we cannot hope to discover the core of our personal identity – who we are and who we were meant to be – without first encountering the One who is both our Creator and King.

I AM GOD'S GOOD CREATION

Genesis tells us God is the Creator who is good and creates good things. What does that say about you and me? As God's good creation, we have a good purpose.

Genesis 1:27-28 tells us, "27 So God created man in His own image; in the image of God He created him; male and female He created them. 28 Then God blessed them, and God said to them, 'Be fruitful and multiply; fill the earth and subdue it; have dominion over the fish of the sea, over the birds of the air, and over every living thing that moves on the earth.'"

At creation, God created Adam and Eve, (and you and me) in his image. This is the basis of our personal identity. It's not how many kids we have or don't have. It's not our stated profession – power executive or stay-at-home mom. Our identity has little to do with our personalities, and even less to do with our mistakes. I'm a victim. I'm a survivor.

We wear all these labels because they make us feel safe. Our identity – who we are in our innermost core – is rooted in the fact that God made us. And when he created us, he made us like him and to be his.

Why did God do this? Why did he get so personally involved in this part of his creation? God shared his likeness with us for two very good reasons: God wanted us to be a *representation* of him and a *representative* of him.

I am a representation of the King

As God's good creation, we are a *representation* of our King. That means God designed us to reflect his abilities – in our capacities to reason, think, express emotion, perceive and create beauty. We reflect God in these areas, and in all these areas, we differ from the rest of the King's creation. No other part of creation bears its Creator's likeness in this way. When we use these abilities, we are a representation of our good King.

I am a representative of the King

But there is another aspect to bearing God's image. Not only are we a representation of our King, but we are his representative, too.

Read Genesis 1:28 again, "Then God blessed them, and God said to them, 'Be fruitful and multiply; fill the earth and subdue it; have dominion over the fish of the sea, over the birds of the air, and over every living thing that moves on the earth.'"

God gave us a very important job, a job that he didn't give to any other part of his creation. Mankind was to function as God's *representative* over the earth – ruling it, having dominion over it. God delegated authority to us. We were intended to be God's sub-regents under *the* King.

In Gen. 2:15, Adam is charged with "tending" and

"keeping" the garden, words used to describe the activity of priests as they serve in the temple (Num. 3:7-8, 8: 25-26). In Gen. 2:18, Eve is called to help Adam accomplish all he had to do. Both were expected to have dominion over the earth and all the animals (Gen. 1:26-28). They were to be servant kings or sub-regents under the King of Kings, stewarding the earth in the King's name. They were supposed to show what life in the King's kingdom looked like – a life of rest as they went about their daily activities.

> **IMAGE OF GOD:** We bear God's image as his *representation* and *representative* on earth. We are crowned in both who we are and what we are called to do.

God, himself, showed Adam and Eve what it looked like to "reign" over the earth. After creating the whole world, God rested on the seventh day, a picture of God reigning over his creation.[4] Because he is the eternal King, God's reign and rest never end. His representatives on earth were intended to point others to the rest he provides.

Today, acting as God's representative on the earth looks a little different than in Adam and Eve's day, but it still entails this aspect of ruling, or resting in God. When God gave you his image, he planned for you to be his representative showing what a restful life in the King's kingdom looks like in whatever sphere he has placed you.

At this point, we must ask ourselves, where is our primary sphere of influence? Is it in the kitchen, around the office water cooler, the classroom, school board, or boardroom? How can we represent our King, showcasing the rest his presence affords regardless of season or circumstance? This is our act of worship.

In my own season of life, representing the King might mean cultivating my home by making it a place of peace and rest despite our chronic busyness and the chaos that often ensues in rearing six-year-old twin boys. It means dealing with my children in the way the King treats his sons – being faithful to love when they are unlovable, extending grace when it's undeserved, and promoting justice during fights and squabbles, tempering them with kindness and mercy. In our family's ministry context, it means opening my home (and heart) willingly and consistently to those in our community who don't know the King. In these acts, no matter how small or mundane, I represent my King to those inside and outside my home.

What does the King's kingdom look like in the office? Undoubtedly, it is a demonstration of the King's character, seeking to enlarge his spiritual family where possible. It looks like doing the best possible job rather than cutting out early. It looks like the humble offering of solutions rather than grumbling shared with coworkers or complaints lodged at the cafeteria. It looks like setting aside selfish ambition through kind words that encourage others in their work. If undertaken with a heart to serve the King, every job or action item becomes an opportunity to demonstrate to a watching world what God envisioned for work when he crowned Adam and Eve in the garden.

In our communities, do our interactions with our neighbors reflect the nature of our service to the King? Do we carefully cultivate connections with those on our street, or do we wait to get out of our car until our garage door shuts behind us to avoid the inconvenience of small-talk? I've been there and done that. Going out of our way to represent the King is especially difficult on long days full of bad news and setbacks. But it is in those moments when we choose joy over fretting that our King and the rest he offers shines the most brilliantly to those around us. We only need to make ourselves available so others can see it.

Engaging neighbors can be daunting when the risk of rejection is high. My friend Joy found a clever way to battle this fear and reach out to her community. She and her husband planted a church in Florida and used the sunny weather to their advantage to reach the lost. They positioned porch furniture in an accessible place in their yard and arranged seating for multiple guests. When someone walked by with their stroller or dog, they were able to offer more than a smile or nod; they offered up a seat and a cold bottle of water. Joy's front porch became a mini-kingdom of Christ, a place of physical rest and community for her neighbors, and she and her husband were its reigning ambassadors. In her yard, wearing flip flops and shorts, the image of God shone bright in Joy. And through simple conversations in the grass, my Joy was able to point her neighbors to the eternal rest of Christ and his kingdom.

Because you bear God's image, you've been crowned as God's masterpiece over all creation. As his daughter, God has tasked you with ruling over creation as his representative, resting in him. The way you live your life should serve as a reflection of the way God lives his and a marker for others to find rest in him (Matt. 11-12).

CHAPTER 1 TAKEAWAYS

I picked Ephesians 2 for our memory passage in this study for several reasons. First, it is one of my favorite passages of Scripture, and second, it hits on so many of the truths we will unpack in this book.

Paul starts off in Eph. 2 by calling us 'children of wrath' or darkness, but you get the sense that this is not the way it was originally supposed to be. We weren't supposed to belong to the darkness. We started off belonging to someone else. You were created by a good Creator to mirror his goodness by doing some very good things in his name. Consider these two takeaways about your personal identity as you begin to memorize Eph. 2.

I have great personal worth

You have personal worth because you were created by a good Creator. Because he created you, you belong to him. You are not just a cog in a wheel. You aren't just a piece of pottery to be collected, put on display, or used at whim only later to be discarded. You were created to be God's child – to look like him, talk like him, walk like him.

Our relationship to our Creator defines our personal worth in unalterable, irrevocable ways. My children belong to me. Because they are related to me, they bear both my name and my image. And because they are mine, I am compelled to cherish, value, and guide them. I do not treat them as objects or trophies of my own success. Instead, they are mine, and they are deeply loved.

But despite belonging to God as his children and his creation, Paul tells us we've chosen another father and another family. Our choice to belong to someone else results in a very real identity change - our lifestyles reflect another father (Eph. 2:1-3). Instead of mirroring a good King and Creator, we mirror a father of deep darkness. But I like the title Scripture gives to those of us who have chosen our Father in heaven again. We are called daughters of the King. Second Corinthians 6:18 says, "I will be a Father to you, and you shall be My sons and daughters, says the LORD Almighty."

The title daughter of the King is not earned, bargained for, or bestowed because of special giftings or good behavior. Zach and Jonah aren't my kids because they've earned it, because I feel sorry for them, or because I am obligated to care for them. They are my children because I helped create them! They belong to me by virtue of being my sons.

Likewise, being a daughter of the King is an enduring

title given to us for no other reason than that we are related to the King - a King who created us and loves us. We are his daughters. And when we are with our Father, dwelling with him, we are at peace. We will never be happier or more "at home" than we are in the presence of our King (Ps. 47:11).

I have great personal purpose

We have worth because we are God's good creation – we belong to Him. That means we are related to him.

Not only do you have great personal worth as a daughter of the King, but you also have a great personal purpose. You were created to reflect the King in what you do and how you're built. God created us to show what life in his kingdom looks like; we are intended to live a life that mirrors God's goodness. Similarly, my own children reflect me to some extent, although sometimes I'd like to think they reflect their earthly father a little more.

But there is even better news! God's purpose for us to live at peace and rest in him doesn't mean we are to be idle or lazy. As his daughter, there is much to do. As the title of this book states, we were created first and foremost for glory – just not necessarily our own. We were created to bring God glory in the way we live. We are intended to show what a life of peace and rest looks like in our King's kingdom, despite circumstances and suffering, despite the victories or losses we endure. We are crowned with purpose.

The crown, biblically speaking, isn't so much a symbol of prestige and entitlement as it is a token of Christ's unmerited kindness given wholeheartedly and humbly to those who will accept it. The crown we wear as women adopted into a royal family doesn't simply signify who we are, but to whom we belong.

In a very real, albeit small way, the crowns we wear as

daughters of the King reflect the nature of the crown of thorns worn by our Lord Jesus as he hung on the cross. The crowns given to us by our Father and King reveal not just our identity, who we are and to whom we belong, but also the mission to which we've been called. This thought is echoed in Eph. 2:10. You are meant to serve God and bring him glory - "walking in the good works he has appointed" for you.

We are ambassadors of the King's throne, and this privilege gives us unfettered access to the throne room of heaven where power, authority, and glory reside. The King has delegated all the force of his throne to us and in making us his servant kings, he has shared his own glory with those of us who have made the King of the world the King of our hearts as well. We were designed for this purpose at the very beginning. Being crowned by the King means much more than enjoying the vestiges and glory of the throne, but knowing the very King himself and being crowned with his royal nature.

I love how author Hannah Anderson phrases this in her book, *Made For More*.

"When Genesis teaches that we are made [in God's image], it is doing more than simply explaining how we came into existence or offering an argument for why we should respect and care for one another. By revealing that we are made in God's image, it is revealing how we are to exist, how we are made to live, and what it means to be human. Being human means sharing God's nature in some way;

being human means living as He lives and doing what He does."[5]

Above all, I want you to finish this chapter knowing that you are special for two reasons. First, you have *great personal worth* simply because you were created by a Good Creator, and second, you have a *great personal purpose* because you were created to live a life at rest in him and reflect God in your everyday activities.

This is much harder than it sounds, right? More often than not, our lives today are no garden. There is family drama, hardships, financial regret. Many of us are desperate to sustain a sense of peace in the face of difficulties and hardships. What gives? In the next chapter, we're going to discover that something has destroyed the bliss God intended for us in the Garden of Eden. And that peaceful and purposeful life now looks like a canvas ripped asunder from its frame.

1. According to the book of Genesis, who is God? Why does it matter if we acknowledge God as the Creator?

2. According to Ps. 29:10-11, what are some of the benefits of living in the King's kingdom?

3. Write down a sentence or two describing who you are. Consider how you've described yourself in your social media profiles. Has Christ changed the way you see or describe yourself to others? How?

4. What do the following verses say about your identity?
   - Isaiah 43:1
   - Romans 8:15
   - Ephesians 1:5
   - Galatians 4:4-7
   - 2 Corinthians 6:18

5. What is your primary area of influence? (office, classroom, home, community, etc.) How can you reflect God in it and show what life in the King's kingdom looks like?

For additional study:

Using a Bible concordance or a site like BibleGateway.com, conduct a word search on the "image of God." In your search, consider how sin impacts the image of God, and how it impacts our relationships. (Think about the way you treat and value others in your home, neighborhood, marriage, church, and place of work.)

CHAPTER 2: DETHRONED

CHAPTER 2 TRUTHS

1) Who is God? God is my Savior.

2) Who am I? I am a sinner, freed from sin in Christ.

In our house, we don't have cable. We get a few basic channels using some rabbit ears, which isn't too annoying if you don't mind a little static during your favorite television program or having to hold your mouth just right as you adjust the antennae. When we do take the time to sit down for a family movie night, we usually turn on Netflix because we don't have to mess with the antennae.

But last summer, my boys became obsessed with *American Ninja Warrior* – an NBC reality television show in which everyday people compete in over-the-top obstacles that would make an Olympic champion's heart race. Each time a competitor failed in their attempt to scale the show's infamous 10-foot vertical wall and plummeted into the giant pool of water waiting below, the boys of the house (husband included) howled with laughter. The static from the rabbit ears didn't deter their merriment a bit.

However, each time we watched the program together, I was a nervous wreck – not because of the heart-pounding feats these athletes must endure – but because of the commercials between the show's segments. My husband and I were constantly turning the TV off at the commercial break, or if one of us can't get to the remote fast enough, we covered the twins' eyes. There are just some things they are not ready to see. There are just some things *I'm* not ready for them to see.

So far in our study of our personal identity in Christ, our story has been exciting and enjoyable. Remember, in each chapter we're asking two key questions: *Who is God?* and *Who am I?* In chapter 1, we uncovered that God is our good Creator. He created everything in the universe for an important purpose: not just to admire his handiwork or pick up a hobby, but so that his creation would mirror his goodness.

As a result, we learned two things about our identity as God's good creation. First, we have great personal *worth,* and second, we have a great personal *purpose* to reflect him as his representative on earth.

Chapter 1 in this book is like the feel-good movie of the year. Chapter 2, however, is going to read like a reality television show. In this chapter, there is drama and there is gore. Some insidious commercials have interrupted our story, and I really want to cover your eyes, but we have to see this.

WHO AM I? I AM A SINNER

Plainly put, the Bible calls us sinners. I like to call sin the "s-word" because in our culture, we don't like to talk about sin because it is a word that implies blame or fault. We would rather blame our troubles or issues on our society, our DNA, our parents, our past, and even our environment. Pointing the finger makes it much easier to watch the bad parts of our lives without having to get up to change the channel.

But the Apostle Paul tells us in Eph. 2:1-3 that we are sinners and are irreparably damaged just like that torn Pablo Picasso painting in the New York Metropolitan Museum of Art. And while we didn't start out that way, we have become broken canvases no longer capable of speaking to the skill of the One who painted us. To add further insult to injury, imagine Pablo Picasso lovingly painting over 1 billion paintings, all of which see ruin at one time or another. Wickedness does not occur in isolation, as if one misstep might more easily be corrected. Sin is a universal epidemic. No thing or person can escape the rips and tears caused by sin. Rather, all humans are united by two things. It doesn't matter if you grew up in privilege or poverty. First, we all share God's image equally, and second, we all have broken God's law equally.

WHAT IS SIN?

- Sin is missing the mark of God's holiness (Rom. 3:23)
- Sin is lawlessness (Rom. 4:7; 1 John 3:4)
- Sin is any act of wickedness (1 Cor. 6:9-10)
- Sin is disobedience (Rom. 5:19)
- Sin is rebellion (Is. 30:1; Eph. 2:3)
- Sin is universal (Rom. 3:23)
- Sin is comprehensive (Mark 7:20-23)

My problem: I have broken God's Law

The Bible uses many words to speak of sin. It can mean we miss the mark of God's standard of holiness (Rom.

3:23). It can mean lawlessness or any act of wickedness (1 Cor. 6:9-10; 1 John 3:4). It can also imply uncleanliness and disobedience (Eph. 2:5, Rom. 5:19). But at its most basic level, Scripture regards sin as rebellion (Is. 30:1; Eph. 2:3). As sinners, we have rebelled against our King and Creator and against his kingdom.

Turn to Gen. 2:16-17. We're going to see that right after God puts Adam in this lush garden and provides everything he needs for a good life, a life of peace and rest with his Creator, God outlines the parameters for Adam to remain there.

Gen. 2:16-17 says, "And the LORD God commanded the man, saying, 'You may surely eat of every tree of the garden, [17] but of the tree of the knowledge of good and evil you shall not eat, for in the day that you eat of it you shall surely die.'" The author is making a very, very important point here: Because God created us and we belong to him, *God alone knows what is good for man* and what is not good for him.[6] Contrary to the world, which views the human heart as the arbiter of right and wrong, Scripture says that only our Creator can know what is best for us and what will be disastrous. The good Creator who created this good world knows what is truly good for us.

God's law, then, is set up to enable man to stay in the garden and enjoy this life of rest with God. It isn't just because God is a cosmic kill joy or because God just really likes rules. I'll be the first one to raise my hand and confess I enjoy rules. But that's not God's heart in giving a law for Adam to uphold. He knows what is best for his creation, what will make it thrive and what will make it die.

Despite knowing God's goodness and the good life he had given them, Adam and Eve choose to break God's commandment. They rebel against his throne. In Gen. 3:4-7, another character enters our story – a serpent who casts doubt on the character of Adam and Eve's King and his good design for his kingdom.

Who is this character? The book of Revelation (the last book of the Bible) tells us this serpent is Satan, a created spiritual being, who is not new to rebellions. Before God created the earth, Satan staged his first coup and rebelled against God in the heavenlies. And although Satan was cast out of heaven along with a host of other beings, he remains at large ruling his own kingdom of darkness (Rev. 12:7).

It is Satan to which Paul refers in our memory passage when he says that we walk according to the "prince of the power of the air" (Eph. 2:1-2). Satan, as evil, always stands against God. But as a created being, like the rest of creation, Satan is subject to God and the rules of his kingdom. However, that doesn't stop him from trying to thwart his good Creator or the goodness of the rest of God's creation. With the creation of the world and God's servant kings, Satan sees his chance to restage his rebellion. So, he takes the form of a serpent and entices Eve to break God's law.

Gen. 3:4-7 gives us some insight into how this cunning deceiver works: "But the serpent said to the woman, 'You will not surely die. [5] For God knows that when you eat of it your eyes will be opened, and you will be like God, knowing good and evil.' [6] So when the woman saw that the tree was good for food, and that it was a delight to the eyes, and that the tree was to be desired to make one wise, she took of its fruit and ate, and she also gave some to her husband who was with her, and he ate. [7] Then the eyes of both were opened, and they knew that they were naked. And they sewed fig leaves together and made themselves loincloths."

So, let's break this rebellion down. Notice what verse 6 says: "So when the woman saw that the tree was good for food, that it was pleasant to the eyes, and a tree desirable to make one wise, she took of its fruit and ate…" (emphasis mine).

The author is pulling our attention to the goodness of creation. Only, instead of God defining what is "good," now we see Eve is determining what is "good" on her own.

In Eve's estimation, the tree is good for three reasons.

1. *It is good to eat.* It has a seemingly good function. It is good for her body.
2. *It is good to look upon.* It has a seemingly good appearance. It is good for pleasure.
3. *It is good for wisdom.* It has seemingly good benefits. It can make her powerful.

Now, these things might be true. The forbidden fruit could very well have been the planet's first "super food," but do you see the danger? God didn't forbid the couple to eat from the tree for any of these reasons; God put his rule into effect so that man might fully enjoy the "good" God created and be protected from death. God put the rule into effect so that man might live life at its best.

In the manner of her tempter, Eve puts herself in God's position when she ate the forbidden fruit, acting as the judge of what is "good" and how she would enjoy that "good" apart from God's provision. And as one crowned by the King to rule in his stead, this is the mightiest act of rebellion. The sub-regent casts off the authority of her King and acts in her own name instead.[7]

In the biblical story, this whole scene is an impending train wreck. There are flashing lights and sirens screaming. Much like a reality television show, you know what's going to happen and yet you just can't tear your eyes away. And ironically, the first couple's quest to determine what constituted both good and evil apart from their King leaves them unable to enjoy the 'good' at all!

Result #1: Sin separates me from God

In Adam and Eve's life, their sin specifically had two main results. Today, sin has the same two consequences. First, *when we break God's law, we are separated from God, our good Creator.* In the rest of Genesis 3, we see some major consequences of sin. The first couple experiences a death in their relationship with God.

Gen. 3:23-24 gives us the snapshot: "23 therefore the LORD God sent him out from the garden of Eden to work the ground from which he was taken. 24 He drove out the man, and at the east of the garden of Eden he placed the cherubim and a flaming sword that turned every way to guard the way to the tree of life."

Adam and Eve's choice to break God's law meant they were exiled from the garden. They are physically driven from the land, but most importantly, they are driven from God's *presence* – their place and source of rest and peace. They experienced a spiritual death – a separation from God. That life of rest for which they were intended is gone. The same is true for you and me today. Because we are sinners, we are separated from God.

Result #2: Sin corrupts the image of God in me

Not only does sin separate us from God, who is Life, secondly, sin corrupts God's image in us. Some of you might be thinking, *"What? That was Eve, okay? Not me. She was the one who messed up! So, why am I getting the blame? I wasn't in the garden. Twenty-first century, remember? Forbidden fruit, ancient history! I had nothing to do with it."* It's a fair question: how do we get lumped in with Eve?

In your small group or personal devotions, I hope you are striving to memorize Eph. 2:1-10. Let's look at this passage because it provides some clues as to how we, too, come to be considered sinners along with Adam and Eve. Eph. 2:1-2 tell us, "And you he made alive, who were dead in trespasses and sins, 2 in which you once walked…"

Oops. So, we are walking in sin, too. Just like Eve, we choose what path to walk on. We are just as guilty of choosing sin as she did. Even if we believe we do more "good" things than "bad" things, we are still sinners because God is the standard for goodness, and we can never live up to that perfect standard.

THE RESULTS OF SIN

- Sin separates me from God (Is. 59:2)
- Sin corrupts God's image in me (Eph. 2:1-2)
- Sin results in death (Rom. 5:12; 6:23)

But what about all those little cute cuddly babies in the world. My friend Meri has what is, quite possibly, the cutest little baby on the planet. Her baby has the biggest and brightest blue eyes. But what makes her so adorable (besides her eyes), are the two juicy little cheeks that frame her sweet smile. Each time I see her, I just want to squeeze those little cheeks off. One can't help but wonder, how could this adorable baby, or any baby for that matter, be considered a sinner separated from God? What crime could a baby commit when they don't even know how to walk or talk?

Well, Paul tells us in Eph. 2 that not only do we *choose* to walk in sin, but we're also *born* into it. In verse 3, he says: "we were by nature deserving of wrath."

So, even if you think *"Well, I may have messed up a couple of times here and there, but what about that lady? Now, SHE'S got probs."* We shouldn't be so hasty because Paul says even if you consider yourself a good person, and you generally try to avoid killing people, which is showing some amazing will power for some of us (especially before our morning coffee), God still considers you a sinner because "you are <u>by nature</u> deserving of wrath" (emphasis mine). That means it is in our nature to sin. Sin started with our first parents (Adam and Eve), and it has been passed down to every human in the history of the world ever since.

So, it doesn't matter if you live in the sanctuary of suburbia or the parched sands of Saudi Arabia, sin is a part of your life because it is first and foremost an internal reality. Sin is a heart problem. We are born with a heart bent toward sin – to think of ourselves first, to want to be first, to want to be the ruler of our lives.

One of the books I like to recommend is *Big Truths for Young Hearts* by Bible scholar and seminary professor Bruce Ware. Intended as a tool for parents to teach their children Christian doctrine, Ware offers accessible illustrations (think Legos) of complicated theological concepts.

In his chapter on sin, Ware explains how sin spreads to all people. He writes: "If you still wonder how we can be sinners before we have sinned, consider this illustration. Would you say that a tree bears apples because it already is an apple tree, or does the tree become an apple tree when it produces its first apple? Well, it is pretty clear. I hope we all would agree that the reason the tree bears apples is because it already has been and is an apple tree. In fact, an apple tree can grow as a small tree for many years before it ever produces its first piece of fruit."[8]

Basically, we are sinners because we have both chosen to walk in sin (sin is hanging off of us like bad fruit – anger, jealously, pride, selfishness, laziness), and we are sinners because we are born into a family of sinners (even before we commit a single act of sin, we are sinners). We have within us this propensity to sin; we are born with a sinful nature. And here's why that distinction is so important. Not only does sin separates us from God (death), but sin also corrupts the image of God in us.

With a corrupted image of God it is impossible to obey God perfectly so that we can reflect his goodness perfectly in our everyday life, to find rest, peace in this life.

Oh, we still bear God's image. We still have value and dignity as his creation. We still bear the responsibilities of representing him as we go about life wearing those crowns he gave us when he created us. We are still tasked with being God's representative here on earth. But this sin nature inside of us now makes us a poor reflection of him. God created us with a bent toward him, but sin makes us bend away from him and toward ourselves. We are rulers unto ourselves who have dethroned the rightful King.

So, who am I? In the plainest terms possible, I am a sinner.

In Paul's words in Ephesians, he says "we are dead" (Eph. 2:1). We have experienced a death and are in need of life. You are a sinner in need of a way to get back into the presence of God, who IS life. I am a sinner in need of some way to restore the image of God within me so I can live the life I was created for.

Okay, you can uncover your eyes now, because this is where our good Creator steps in. He created us once, and now he is now going to fix us, recreate us.

WHO IS GOD? GOD IS MY SAVIOR

Despite Adam and Eve's sin, God shows them mercy. Before God kicks them out of the garden, he gives them something.

Gen. 3:21 says, "And the LORD God made for Adam and for his wife garments of skins and clothed them."

God gives Adam and Eve clothing for this new life they will have to endure apart from him. Before sin, Adam and Eve had no need for clothes. (This also might be a cover your eyes moment.) They didn't need clothes because they knew no shame. They were God's good creation, but sin changes all that. Guilt and shame enter the equation changing the way they look at each other and themselves. And in an attempt to cover their shame, they try to fashion their own covering or clothing from fig leaves (Gen. 3:7).

But God provided clothes for them to protect them in their exile. This is an act of mercy. But there's something else here because this could very well be the first animal sacrifice. God gave them tunics of skin. There had to be a death in order for Adam and Eve to receive God's mercy. This demonstrates that sin is real, it is ugly, and it is costly. Sin costs a life.

Ultimately, it is God who pays that price on our behalf. He provides the sacrifice for our sins. He is our Savior. And we see that hinted here in Gen. 3:21 when he provides for Adam and Eve when he wasn't obligated to do so. God could have said, *"See ya, wouldn't want to be ya! Don't let the flaming sword hit ya on your way out."*

But instead, he chooses to pay that costly price on their behalf. So, how does he do that? How does he provide for our sins? Well, Genesis gives us a hint.

God saves me from sin through his Son

Look back at Gen. 3:15, and let me paint for you the backdrop behind this verse. Adam and Eve have broken God's law, and God is revealing to them what the consequences of their choice to sin will be. God is speaking to them, and he's also speaking to the serpent – that crafty guy who deceived Eve into believing God wasn't good and was withholding good things from her, and that she could experience goodness apart from this good God.

Here's what God has to say in Gen. 3:15: "I will put enmity between you and the woman, and between your offspring and her offspring; he shall bruise your head, and you shall bruise his heel."

So, let me explain this passage a little more. This passage is one of the most famous passages in the Bible because it is the first time in Scripture that we have the promise of our salvation. Gen. 3:15 spells out how God is going to provide for us and make us right once again.

These verses reveal that a cosmic battle is going to take place between the serpent and the woman – between her seed and his seed. This battle will continue for generations, but here's how the battle will end. God promises to send someone to conquer sin once and for all. This person he is sending is going to be born from "the woman." He will come from Eve, as her "seed" or offspring.

God intends for a real, live descendent of Eve to come and conquer sin by conquering the serpent. This conqueror will deliver a fatal blow to Satan – a blow to the head. But not before sustaining an injury himself; the serpent "shall bruise His heel."

Now, the writer of Genesis does not give us many details. There is no spoiler alert in this passage: hey, this is Jesus of Nazareth! The writer just drops the bomb that God is going to provide salvation from sin. And, most importantly, it is coming through a human.

However, we know the full story of Christ. Jesus is born of a human, lives a perfect life on planet earth, and then dies a painful and agonizing death on the cross in our place. His heel is crushed, if you will. But we know this act is not eternally fatal because he rose again on the third day and vanquishes death, evil, the serpent, and all of the serpent's seed forever.

Paul tells us in Eph. 2 that God saves us from sin through Christ.

Listen to the words of Eph. 2:4: "⁴ But God, being rich in mercy, because of the great love with which he loved us, ⁵ even when we were dead in our trespasses, made us alive together with Christ–by grace you have been saved..."

The person he promised to send to conquer death and sin was Christ – the Son of God who was a real person, a Son of Eve, who walked and talked and breathed on this earth just like us.

Now, look at the result, what comes out of Christ's death and his conquering of sin.

Because of Christ, Paul says in Ephesians 2:6-7 that we are made to sit "⁶ in the heavenly places in Christ Jesus, ⁷ so that in the coming ages he might show the immeasurable riches of his grace in kindness toward us in Christ Jesus."

Remember, when the good Creator made us, he designed us to rule – to reign on the earth in his name. He crowned us for glory, but we did a sorry job with that, and we were kicked out of the kingdom if you will. In Eph. 2, we are told that we've been restored back to our original post, our job if we acknowledge his Son as our Savior. Because of Christ, we are hired back, and the image of God within is being fully restored.

If you were to keep reading in Eph. 2, you'd hear these words in verses 13-14: "[13] But now in Christ Jesus you who once were far off have been brought near by the blood of Christ. [14] For he himself is our peace, who has made us both one and has broken down in his flesh the dividing wall of hostility."

The NKJV translates verse 14: "and has broken down the middle wall of separation…"

We are sinners, both born into sin and willing participants, and because of that, we were separated from God. But in Christ that separation is gone. We are back dwelling with our Good Creator. We are freed from sin through Christ.

In chapter 3, we will look at *how* we are actually freed from sin through Christ. But right now, I want you to know that it is God who planned it all for us – this rescue project, this restoration.

In this sense, you can know with 100 percent certainty that God is your Savior.

CHAPTER 2 TAKEAWAYS

I can only find lasting rest and joy in God

We will never know lasting rest and peace outside of Christ. Whatever it is we are searching for – validation, escape, pleasure, affection, recognition, independence – we will never be more fulfilled or more at peace than when we are restored back to God. He IS Peace. He IS Life. He IS rest (Eph. 2:13-14). Kingdom rest comes only to hearts and lives made right by a restored relationship to the King of Kings (Matt. 11:26-27; 12:9-14).

I'm not trying to be dramatic here; I'm being pragmatic. God created us for a purpose, to be like him and do what he does, and when we are fulfilling that purpose, we will experience true joy and rest regardless of circumstances.

One of my boys, Jonah, has a favorite story he loves for me to read. It's an adaptation of an Aesop fable about a dog who steals a steak from his master's table and on his escape route he passes over a bridge crossing a stream. Looking down into the stream, the dog is enticed by the image of another dog holding a steak in his mouth. Unaware that it is his own reflection in the water, the dog drops his own steak to grab hold and steal the steak in the other dog's mouth. His greed ensures he loses both dinners.

As Eve found out, we forfeit the good blessings of fulfillment and belonging when we choose to pursue and grab ahold of other things that seem better. However, in the end, the "goodness" they seek proves to be a mere illusion. And before we know it, like the greedy dog in Aesop's fable, we've lost all the good blessings given to us by our good God: life, peace, joy, fulfillment, rest.

In chapter 1, we learned that our Creator is good, and what he does is good. So, we must also trust that what God has for us is good, and that he is powerful enough to bring good out of the messes and pits in our lives. When we trust that he is good, his ways are good, and his words to us are good, we will find unending storehouses of rest and joy.

I can only be freed from sin by Christ

If God created us and knows what's best for us, then we

must trust that he knows how to fix us. And most importantly, we can have confidence that he is willing to fix us!

Christ is the only way for us to get back into the presence of God. Christ is the only way God's image in us can be restored back to its full glory. And in chapter 3, we'll find out *how* that all happens.

1. Describe Eve's decision to disobey God's Law in Genesis 3:6. Ultimately, what was Eve saying about herself and God when she broke God's Law?

2. Is there an area of your life that is hard to accept God's way is best or good for us?(Some examples might include: family life, marriage, dating, work issues, parenting, relationships, future decisions, etc.)

3. Would you describe yourself as a sinner? Why or why not?

4. What do the following verses say about sin?
    *   Proverbs 14:12
    *   Isaiah 59:2
    *   Romans 3:23
    *   Romans 6:23

5. What does Romans 5:12 say about us?

6. What hope does Gen. 3:15 give us? What does this hope mean for the corrupted image of God within us?

For additional study:

Using a Bible dictionary, look up the entry for "sin." Compare and contrast how the Old Testament and New Testament talk about sin. Consider where sin springs from and list some of the consequences of sin witnessed in our daily lives.

CHAPTER 3: ROYAL ROBES

CHAPTER 3 TRUTHS

1) Who is God? God is my Righteous Judge.

2) Who am I? I am declared right in Christ.

Since 1689, Ede & Ravenscroft have been the appointed robe makers and tailors to the British monarchy spanning back to the coronation of Edward VII and his wife Queen Alexandra. Only one of a few companies granted three royal warrants to supply the monarch with goods or services, the handmade robes produced by Ede & Ravenscroft use silk, satin, damask, cloth-of-gold (cloth spun with gold) and the finest ermine. At the lavish coronation of George IV, the royal robe makers also outfitted a host of court officials including 48 Knights Grand Cross of the Order of the Bath and 100 Knights Commander of the Bath with robes and mantles.

But perhaps the most famous of the royal robe maker's regalia is the six-foot long purple velvet cloak worn by Her Majesty Queen Elizabeth II on her coronation day, June 2,

1953. Following ceremonial guidelines, the rich train was trimmed in white ermine and its sides embroidered with gold bullion thread designed with ears of wheat, leaves and stalks intertwining its full length. The design culminated at the end of the train with a solid gold embroidered crown.

The richness and intricacy of the Queen's purple velvet coronation robe is the type of robe we envision rulers to wear when they have claimed both their crown and throne. But following ceremonial tradition, several robes are featured during a coronation service. Queen Elizabeth wore four.

Perhaps the most interesting and symbolic of the coronation garments is the Colobium Sindonis, which is Latin for "shroud tunic." As a sleeveless linen shift, this robe stands in stark contrast to the lush velvets and gold silks of those attending the royal ceremony. Its simplicity underscores the ruler's commitment and duty to divest him or herself of worldly vanity and as such, presents a symbolic picture of one standing unadorned before the King of Kings.

At Queen Elizabeth's coronation, six maids helped the Queen change her robes and remove all her jewelry. Covered in the linen Colobium Sindonis, the unembellished Elizabeth looked more like a simple servant than a privileged and powerful heir to the throne. Next, over this white robe, the Queen donned a golden Supertunica, the same golden cloak worn by kings before her. Full of meaning, these two robes relate to priestly garments and are worn during the investiture part of the coronation ceremony. They are poignant reminders of the divine position and solemn obligation under which rulers live and the divine power in which they were invested.

With her shoulders encircled in the golden robe, Queen Elizabeth waited to receive her crown. The Archbishop recited this liturgy taken from Is. 61:10: "Receive this Imperial Robe, and the Lord your God endue you with knowledge and wisdom, with majesty and with power from on high; the Lord clothe you with the robe of righteousness, and with the garments of salvation. Amen."

The royal regalia of the British monarchy are more than lovely garments worn for a special occasion. Whether they are made from rich velvet or stark linen, royal robes offer two weighty reminders: first, one's rule must be pursuant of righteousness, and second, a ruler is dependent on divine intervention to achieve it.[9]

In chapter 1, we learned that God is the good Creator, and everything he does and makes is good. Even the purpose for which we are created is good; we are to mirror God's goodness.

In chapter 2, we discovered that sin corrupted the goodness of God in us. We are, as Paul tells us in Ephesians 2:1-2, sinners. We have rebelled against the throne of the King of Kings. However, this news ends on a note of hope: God promises not to leave us in our condition. God is our Savior.

As we enter into chapter 3, we discover exactly how God comes to be our Savior and what that means for both our future and present circumstances.

WHO IS GOD? GOD IS MY RIGHTEOUS JUDGE

God judges my sin

As the King par excellence, God rules his kingdom in complete righteousness. He is our righteous Judge, a title we see repeatedly in the Scriptures. One place this title is found is Psalm 9:8: "And He will judge the world in righteousness; He will execute judgment for the peoples with equity."

As a righteous Judge, not only does God act righteously, but he also punishes unrighteousness in his kingdom. As the a righteous ruler, God guarantees that justice will prevail in and over all circumstances – in the stories of domestic abuse victims in high-profile NFL marriages, to jailed civilians, pilots, and journalists beheaded by terrorists and slave traders like ISIS/ISIL. Our world needs justice, and God's Word promises that wrongdoers will be held accountable (Ps. 37).

For those born and raised in the U.S., living under the rule of a monarch is a foreign concept. However, I think we can all agree that if we are going to be ruled, we would want our ruler to be righteous. I know very few who would enjoy the rule of one known to overlook injustice and refuse to pursue offenders.

In her coronation oath, Her Majesty Queen Elizabeth II was asked by the Archbishop to pledge to use her power to "cause Law and Justice, in Mercy, to be executed in all [her] judgments." Specifically, the Queen was asked to uphold the laws of God and the gospel.[10]

Look up Galatians 3:10. If you're new to Galatians, I'll give you a quick synopsis of this little book. Galatians was written by the Apostle Paul to all the churches he helped found during his missionary journeys to the region of Galatia.

Paul wrote to encourage the younger believers in these churches because they were confused about the word "righteous" and how they, too, could attain righteousness. You see, these new believers were being told by a group in the church that they were responsible for fixing themselves and their sin problem.

Specifically, this group was telling young believers that they had to *be* righteous before God would accept them. They said righteousness came through keeping all the laws of the Old Testament, and if they kept all of God's laws, then they would be "righteous" (Gal. 2:4-21).

And Paul says flat out, *"Nope. That's wrong."* Here's why. Gal. 3:10 tells us, "[10] For all who rely on the works of the law are under a curse, as it is written: 'Cursed is everyone who does not continue to do <u>everything</u> written in the Book of the Law'" (NIV, emphasis mine).

Law, here, means the first five books of the Bible. Now, in those first five books there are over 600 laws – laws that govern diet, business, social customs, marriage, and relationships. Laws on everything from how to cook your food to how to how to wear your hair (Lev. 11 and 19 provide some good samples).

Bottom line: there are too many rules in God's Law to follow perfectly - a truth I learned rather painfully when I took the twins to an indoor bounce house gym. Located inside a ginormous warehouse, there were no less than 10 different bounce houses for the boys to choose from. Some had slides, others had climbing walls. One was a giant pirate ship, and one looked like a wrestling ring – all things loved and cherished by six-year-old boys.

When we walked in, you should have seen their faces: pure elation. But I watched that joy quickly fade from their eyes as one of the employees began to explain the rules. There were no less than 50, all designed to protect anyone from getting hurt, and so it seemed, from having any amount of fun.

And as the employee stood there, obstructing their view of bounce house bliss, reciting all the rules – no running, no pushing, no screaming (really? It's a warehouse), no climbing on the walls – the twins realized this place wasn't as promising as they first thought. And for mom, too, because I knew there was no way they were going to remember all those rules. No matter how hard they tried to toe the line, I knew one of my children would inevitably break one of those good rules.

And they did.

And we left.

Because God is righteous; he always does the right thing, morally, ethically. It is through his Laws, that we come to know of the perfections of God's holiness, but it also through God's Law that we see the magnitude of our sin and unrighteousness (Rom. 7:7-12; see also Gal. 3:19).

WHAT MAKES GOD SO RIGHTEOUS?

God always does the right thing (character) and always does the right thing toward me (activity).

In Galatians, Paul tells these new believers, *"Guess what — you are anything but righteous, so stop playing!"* Trying to live by the Law, no matter how good those laws are, makes for a cursed life, Paul says. And God didn't intend for us to live a life of curses, did he? He created us to live a life of rest in him. He created us to live a life mirroring his goodness, his righteousness.

Now, up till this point, you might be tempted to thinking: *"How boring! Always doing the right thing! Ugh!"* Think of my twins in the bounce house. The thought of having to follow all those rules suddenly sucked all the joy out that excursion. But when Scripture tells us that God always does the right thing, it means specifically, *that God always does the right things toward us!*

And as sinners who have rebelled against him, what would be the right thing to do to us? God's righteousness compels him to judge our sin. He is the perfect King because he always judges sin. Think about an earthly judge. How righteous would he be if he swept a crime under the rug or looked the other way over a murder? He wouldn't be very righteous if he refused to preside over a trial, allowing a criminal to get away. In our broken world today, this can and does happen among our leaders.

Think about criminals who walk free based on a technicality. It doesn't matter if it was a police misstep or a judicial loophole, when a criminal who is undoubtedly guilty and has committed a terrible crime doesn't have to pay a price for his wrongdoing, something deep down inside of us knows that it's wrong.

Because God is the righteous Judge, first and foremost, he must do the right thing toward us; he must judge our sin.

But when we say God is righteous, and he does the right thing toward us, we mean more than simply God *judges* our sin, we also mean that God *pardons* my sin.

God pardons my sin

God judges our sin, but he also pardons our sin. And you might be wondering, *"Well, what's so righteous about that? Letting a bad guy off the hook doesn't sound fair. It doesn't really sound like justice was had."*

But when Scripture calls God righteous, it is calling our attention to the fact that God is always faithful to his promises. Ultimately, God's righteousness means *he does the right thing toward us*. He judges sin and pardons us at the same time according to his promises, and it is his righteousness that accomplishes both.

In the previous chapter, we left our session knowing that God promised to provide for our sins. When Adam and Eve sinned they experienced a death; they were separated from God. But God, who is good and merciful and righteous, made a way for them to continue to live despite their sin. Before God kicked the dynamic duo out of the garden, he provided a covering for their shame and guilt. Remember, he killed an animal and gave them the skins to wear to cover their shame.

Let me tell you about animal skins. They stink! I don't care how long an animal has been dead, you can never ever get the stink off it. While traveling overseas, my husband, Jonathan, bought an animal skin from a street vendor in a small alley lining the shops behind our apartment. After some heated haggling, he emerged from that dark corner the victor. He held the animal skin high in the air to show me like a professional wrestler brandishing his championship belt after besting his opponent. (The chicken that I am, I had chosen to wait in the safety of the sunlight across the street.) Even when I got a closer look at the skin, I remained skeptical of his victory because despite his attempts to reassure me of the depth of his bargaining skills, my husband still couldn't tell me what kind of animal he had purchased. Neither of us had ever seen anything like it. The animal was only identifiable as a hairy mammal, and worse still, it wreaked of dust and dried skin and all things indelicate.

Most of the time I kept the hairy beast tucked away in a closet, but each time we moved, I was reminded of how much I hated that animal skin. We moved our mystery friend across oceans, across states, from house to house, and each time I re-discovered it in an attic or dark closet, it scared the heck out of me. I'd grab it with two fingers and fling it into a box because, primarily, it STUNK! It didn't matter how many years we had it, the scent of what that animal once was never faded.

Now, think about Adam and Eve. Don't you think Adam and Eve, as they are wearing those freshly-killed animal skins and feeling that rough skin rub against them, were reminded of the of cost their sin? The dusty and earthy aroma of the fur and dried matter were a far cry from the robes God must have envisioned around his subjects' shoulders. Instead, the furs they wore were poignant and heavy reminders of God's judgment and provision.

TO REDEEM: To buy someone out of slavery, even at a very high price.

That was the purpose of the Old Testament sacrifices: to remind the people of the cost of their sin and who provided the covering for it. The sacrifices were a messy and graphic reminder that God keeps his promises to his people. God proves himself to be the righteous Judge who acts rightly toward us in another way, a better way.

Gal. 3:13 says, "[13] Christ redeemed us from the curse of the law by becoming a curse for us, for it is written: 'Cursed is everyone who is hung on a pole'" (NIV). The NKJV and ESV paint in some more details: "...cursed *is* everyone who hangs on a tree," a reference to the wood that was used to form the cross on which Jesus would die.

So, this is how God can pardon people who don't deserve to be pardoned. This is how he can pardon us without becoming unrighteous or neglecting justice or right and wrong.

Verse 13 says God pardons us by "redeeming" us. This word redeem is very interesting. It means to pay a price in order to secure the release of something or someone. It is, at its very core, a term that whispers justice because it conveys the idea of paying a price in order to free someone.

Many of us know very little of the horrors of physical slavery. In this age, the slavery from which we are "redeemed" is a spiritual slavery, yet no less horrifying in its effects and end. We are chained to our sins, and we can't stop sinning. In Gal. 5:19-21, Paul gives us quite a descriptive list of our sins. He says, "The acts of the flesh are obvious: sexual immorality, impurity and debauchery; [20] idolatry and witchcraft; hatred, discord, jealousy, fits of rage, selfish ambition, dissensions, factions [21] and envy; drunkenness, orgies, and the like. I warn you, as I did before, that those who live like this will not inherit the kingdom of God."

Parts of that list might sound like your family's Sunday ride to church or even a holiday meal with relatives - discord, jealousy, fits of range, selfish ambitions. But whether they are sibling spats or grievous sins committed against us, our hearts tell us this is not the way we were intended to live. We were meant to reign and rest, keeping God's Law, but now we find ourselves unfit for the throne because of all these crimes listed against us.

But God, as the perfect Ruler, provides a way for us to be his servant kings once again. He sends his Son, who is born of a virgin, to earth. And this Son, lives a perfect life. He doesn't break a single law of God, not one. He lives perfectly and shows us what true humanity was intended to look like – what it looks like when a man (or woman) lives their life mirroring God's goodness, living and walking in righteousness.

And instead of getting all the praises for what he did right, Christ dies on the cross for what we did wrong. He takes our seat on death row and is executed instead of us. Through his death we are redeemed, bought back at great personal cost, and are freed from sin.

And the result is this: when God looks at us, he no longer sees us wearing our tattered rags of sin, but gleaming robes of righteousness. Isaiah 61:10, which figured into the Queen Elizabeth's coronation, says, "I will rejoice greatly in the LORD, My soul will exult in my God; For He has clothed me with garments of salvation, He has wrapped me with a robe of righteousness, As a bridegroom decks himself with a garland, And as a bride adorns herself with her jewels."

Using another metaphor, you could think of it like a bank account. One day, you go to the mall (or online, in my case) and make some very poor decisions. These poor decisions lead to a terrible reality: an over-drafted bank account. And while over-drafting your account once or twice won't get you sent to jail or the electric chair, it still means you have some difficult consequences to bear. You have a debt that you are unable to repay, and you are left with no choice but to work to earn extra money to pay back your debts, your mistakes.

But here is the rub. Sometimes, no matter how hard we try to work to save up, we just can't seem to get ahead. We keep sinning, and that money we've worked to tuck away won't cover all our retail regrets. And before we know it, we're in debt again! It's a rat race!

The false teachers in the Galatian churches were giving out some very fraudulent advice on debt and sin. They were telling the new believers among them, *"work hard enough, and you can eliminate your debts all by yourself."*

If these heretics lived in the 21st century, they'd say things like:

You've got to clean yourself up before you cross the doorstep of the church.

You've got to go to church EVERY WEEK, every day to be spiritual enough.

You've got to say your prayers and read the Bible every day or God won't listen to you. And if you fall behind in your Bible reading plan, you might as well give up.

You've got to give a certain amount of money to the church to be a good Christian.

You've got to follow every rule and not ever mess up again. I'm watching you.

No running.

No punching.

No screaming.

No climbing on the walls.

But here's the problem. Since God is the standard for righteousness, we can never do enough to fill up our bank account again. Our sin problem is so great, our debt is so high – remember, sin is costly. Even the best of our good deeds look like "dirty rags" to our perfect King and Judge (Is. 64:6).

Knowing we could never pay off our debt, God allowed Jesus to pay that debt for us. Our debt is death, so he allowed Jesus to die in our place. So, our bank accounts are in the black once again. And all our debts are credited to Christ's account.

It's like this: we've exchanged bank accounts with the world's richest person. His account is ours, and our account is now his. Scholars call this "the Great Exchange." The righteous Judge declares Christ punishable for our sin and declares us righteous instead.

Actually there is a more specific term for this exchange. It is called justification. We are declared right, or justified, by God. There are two components to this act. First, I am declared right because *my sins are credited to Christ*. And second, I am *declared right because Christ's righteousness* is credited to me. In Christ, God both declares us right and treats us as right.

WHO AM I? I AM DECLARED RIGHT

I am declared right because my sins are credited to Christ

So, how does this exchange work? Paul says one word - faith. Faith is how we are declared right. Gal. 3:11 says, "[11] Clearly no one who relies on the law is justified before God, because 'the righteous will live by faith' (NIV).

What kind of faith is Paul talking about? Just faith in general? Faith in people? Just the believe-in-yourself kind of faith? If you were to go back farther to Gal. 2:16, you'd hear Paul answer the question of what kind of faith makes us right. He writes, "We know that a person is not justified by the works of the law, but by faith in Jesus Christ. So we, too, have put our faith in Christ Jesus that we may be justified by faith in Christ and not by the works of the law, because by the works of the law no one will be justified" (emphasis mine).

In order to be declared right by God, you must accept by faith the price that Christ paid on the cross for your sin.

It is not just enough to know about Jesus. To go to church a few times and hear some stories about him or God. It is not enough to have faith that things will work out if you're good and kind to others. We must exercise a specific faith in the person of Jesus Christ and what he did for us on the cross in order to be declared debt-free and for all those minuses to be removed from our bank statement.

Before we step into Christ's precious gleaming robes, we must first accept his work on the cross in our place. We must stand before him as we are, displaying our need for his robes. In the same way that Queen Elizabeth set aside the glitter and pomp of her royal robes to don the plain white linen of her Colobium Sindonis, we too, must come before God bare of pretense. While there is no literal robe for us to wear in this process of trust, we must clothe ourselves with the reminder that there is no good deed lovely enough to provide a truly defensible covering or hiding place from judgment against our sin. We must come to God as we are, acknowledging the state of our own self-constructed coverings and our need of his righteous robes.

I am declared right because Christ's righteousness is credited to me

After we come to this honest expression of faith, Christ rushes in and gives us his gleaming, golden robes of salvation. We become encircled with his righteousness. This is what God sees when you become his daughter. He sees the perfect work of his Son on your behalf.

Herein lies the second element of being declared right. When Christ died on the cross in our place, not only did he take on our debt (death from sins), but he filled our bank account up with something new. Gal. 2:20 says, "[20] I have been crucified with Christ; it is no longer I who live, but Christ lives in me; and the life which I now live in the flesh I live by faith in the Son of God, who loved me and gave

Himself for me."

When Christ died in our place, he gave us his life – a life of righteousness. He filled up our bank accounts with his funds, his resources. And it is from this rich bank account that we can now operate and live our life.

That's what Paul means when he says in verse 16, "it is no longer I who live, but Christ lives in me…" In Christ, we exchange our past for a new future. In Christ, we exchange an old way of life for a new one. So, whatever good things come out of my life after I've been declared right aren't from me, they are due to Christ's works in me.

The Galatians were being told that it was the works of their hands that made them righteous. But Christ says, *"No, have faith that I am going to do those works in you!"*

Pushing this truth further, Paul points out to the Galatian churches the story of Abraham – a patriarch of the faith in the Old Testament, a man to whom God made the very same promise that he made to Eve – that one of his descendants one day would provide for their sins.

WHAT IS JUSTIFICATION?

My sins are credited to Christ and Christ's righteousness is credited to me.

Listen to what he says in Gal. 3:6: "So also Abraham believed God, and it was credited to him as righteousness." We are credited righteousness when we choose to trust in God to provide for our sins. And here's the result: Christ's destiny becomes our destiny. Let's recap by pulling our Scripture memory verse into this, Ephesians 2:1-10. In this passage, we see the results of this great exchange and how our destiny aligns with Christ's destiny.

Beginning in Eph. 2:4, Paul says, "4 But God, who is rich in mercy, because of His great love with which He loved us,

⁵ even when we were dead in trespasses, made us alive together with Christ (by grace you have been saved), and raised us up together…"

So, in this great exchange we go from death to life. We were dead in sins, and then in Christ, we are made alive. We are raised – just like Christ was – to live a new type of life in Him.

Paul continues in 2:6 with, "…and made us sit together in the heavenly places in Christ Jesus..."

In this exchange, we go from a position of disgrace and shame to the highest position of honor – in Christ we're remade to rule with him, seated in the heavenly places in Christ Jesus.

In 2:7, we learn, "⁷ that in the ages to come He might show the exceeding riches of His grace in His kindness toward us in Christ Jesus." In this great exchange, we go from a position of a debtor to a position of great wealth – in Christ we're shown exceeding or incomparable riches of God's grace.

And because we have Christ's righteousness in our accounts, we can walk in those "good works" which God created for us (Eph. 2:10). So, not only am I snatched from death, but I'm given a new type of life. Not only am I set free from past sins, but I'm given Christ's righteousness.

Christ's destiny truly becomes our destiny. We were created to walk in God's glory and after we are justified in Christ, we are given the privilege of sharing in Christ's glory. These are the exceeding riches of God's grace in his kindness toward us: instead of squashing a rebellious regent he chooses to crown us, to robe us in the finest regalia, and give us a share in the kingdom destiny of his own heir.

CHAPTER 3 TAKEAWAYS

My justification is both a past event and present reality

So, you might understand that at the cross, a point in real time, real history, your sins were credited to Christ and his righteousness was credited to you. But what about the future? What happens if you mess up or break one of God's rules next week or tomorrow?

I can tell you right now, despite being declared right by Christ, I'm still going to mess up. I'm still going to lose it when my kids drop popsicles on the floor and leave it for me to clean up. The same goes for you. You might be tempted to get those answers for that math test from a friend or grumble in your heart when your coworker gets a promotion slated for you. So, what then? Do your accounts go into debt again? Does Christ have to die again in order for you to remain debt-free?

We are still going to mess up. It is inevitable, but this is what I want you to take away: Christ's sacrifice is a better sacrifice. The Israelites had to make sacrifices daily and yearly for their sins (Lev. 16; Heb. 7:27). But when Christ took our place, he became the perfect sacrifice. No other sacrifices were needed ever again, no matter how many times we mess up.

How can this be so? Because Christ is eternal, and what he does is eternal. When he died on the cross, he became that one time, eternal sacrifice for our sins. That means Christ's sacrifice covers our sin from eternity past and into eternity future. However you mess up next week, Christ's blood is perfect enough to cover it.

Does that mean we can live how we see fit, sinning a whole bunch and never having to pay the consequences? Unfortunately, the answer is no. There are earthly consequences to sin. You murder someone, you go to jail. You hurt and lie to your family, your relationships suffer. You overspend at Christmas, you're going to have a tight January. But if we are truly living by faith, we will desire to walk in Christ's righteousness. The more we taste, see, and experience God's grace, the more we will want to pursue it.

We are going to want to walk in those good deeds God has planned for us, as Paul says in our Scripture verse (Eph. 2:10).

But speaking of the past: if there are specific things you are still holding onto, don't. Christ's blood covers them even if there are earthly consequences that must still play out. When we hold onto past mistakes, we are saying that the cross wasn't big enough to bear the guilt and shame of our past. When we hold onto past mistakes and misjudgments, we are saying that Christ's blood wasn't pure enough, perfect enough to buy us back from our sin.

When we feel tempted to go back to those lies and tempted to return to our old way of life (our old account), now we can make withdrawals from our new spiritual bank account, an account we can trust will never run out because God's love and mercy never runs out. Christ's righteousness can't run out because he is eternal.

My justification sets me free to love

The best place to discover how deep Christ's love actually runs is in the home. I don't care where you live or how great your state is, there is no perfect home and there is no perfect family. Among my friends I count divorcees, widows, and single women who have found their families plagued by financial regret, relationship trauma, abuse, and more. Thankfully, for those who know Christ, their future shines brighter than their past. But it is those friends who choose to walk in love and grace in present and trying circumstances that awe me the most.

On her wedding day, Rachel (not her real name) became a wife and the mother of a toddler at the same time. Rachel's husband had a daughter born from a previous marriage that had disintegrated due to the sin of his former wife. And despite the big transition, Rachel has soared in her new role as wife and mother. But life is often tumultuous for this young family as the former wife is plagued with mental stability. Rachel and her family often feel like they are riding a roller-coaster of demands and trickery. In most homes, the situation would garner resentment and gossip, but my friend has taken measures to walk in righteousness. Rachel and her husband do not bad-mouth their daughter's mother within earshot. They persistently teach their little one about God's love, even while "unteaching" her ungodly habits she picks up in her mother's home.

When I see my friend Rachel, I know without a doubt that justification is surely a past and future reality, but most importantly, it impacts our present in a powerful way. Each day, Rachel awakes, she is presented with the choice of two wardrobes – one of flesh and one of Spirit. The choice is difficult but so important for those who claim to wear the King's crown and robes.

Look at how Paul finishes his letter to the Galatians. This letter was meant to encourage these new believers to focus their lives on Christ's work in them rather than their works – what they are doing or what others are doing. Gal. 5:13 says, "For you were called to freedom, brothers. Only do not use your freedom as an opportunity for the flesh, but through love serve one another."

Paul says: our justification means we are free now to "serve one another humbly in love" (as the NIV puts it). That's what God, as our good Creator, created us to do, to mirror God's goodness so that when others see us, they see our good God. And God, as our righteous Judge, paid the costly price for our sin so that we could set about to do those things for which we were originally intended, to rule in the way we were intended and share in the glory he desired to give us. Justification means we are redeemed and made righteous, yes, but so that we can love others by serving them.

Here is how author Elyse Fitzpatrick puts it in her book,

Found in Him:

"Because of the justification already freely bestowed on us, we are free to serve our neighbors in love. I am free to serve my neighbor because I don't need to demand my rights – I have everything I need in Christ. I am free to serve my neighbor because I don't need to be respected – Jesus knows exactly who I am, and yet he has given me the position of his queen. I don't need your success and love or approbation or support to make me into a person of worth. My identity is that, right now, I am more than I could ever dream. Justification by grace through faith frees me to take my eyes off how I'm doing (and how you're doing) and look to Jesus, who will place neighbors before me who need to be loved today."[11]

Our justification means we can love our neighbors the way God has loved us – unconditionally, wholeheartedly, intentionally. Our justification means we are armed with resources in our account - those fruits of God's Spirit mentioned here in this letter: "But the fruit of the Spirit is love, joy, peace, forbearance, kindness, goodness, faithfulness, [23] gentleness and self-control" (Gal. 5:22-23).

Those are the resources of righteousness that are put into our account by Christ. When we face an issue where we must choose between honoring ourselves or honoring God, those are the resources we are now free to draw from.

Those people in our life that are incredibly hard to love, we can love them with Christ's love instead of nursing our pride. Those circumstances that just keep coming and from which we can't seem to catch a break, we can face the future with joy and peace instead of grumbling and fear.

That friend or family member who disappointed us time and time again, we can now bear with them, even restraining our speech with gentle words instead of letting bitterness creep in. Those are the resources from which we are now free to draw.

Those good works that God created us to walk in, we

can now do so through Him, with his equipping. Are we going to mess up? Yes, but that's when we can fight back the guilt and shame, knowing that we are already justified, and we can draw forgiveness and joy from that spiritual bank account again.

Wearing Christ's righteous robes means we can trust in his work on our behalf. We can let go of the fear of messing up or not being good enough because Christ is enough for us. We no longer need to rely on our own strength to get through the mess. The same prophet who spoke of our new wardrobe also warned us against the temptation of returning to our old garments. Isaiah 64:6 says, "For all of us have become like one who is unclean, And all our righteous deeds are like a filthy garment..." It doesn't matter how many good deeds we perform (going to church, reading our Bible, giving to the poor), it is as though we are still wearing dirty rags, the prophet says.

Each and every day when we awake, we must choose from which closet we'll select our spiritual clothing. Will we choose to put on Christ's righteousness robes or the dirty rags of our attempts to keep the Law? Christ's robes are made from fabrics finer than any royal robe maker can weave. They do not wear out. They do not rip. They are made from the eternal thread of his grace and love. Christ's robes of righteousness should be our everyday uniform of choice. And for those of us who choose to live based on faith, we will discover that one day those robes will no longer be borrowed threads.

1. What does Psalm 9:8 tell us about God? Who is he and what does he do?

2. Which truth is easier for you to accept: God's righteousness requires him to punish my sin or God's righteousness compels him to pardon my sin? Why?

3. According to Ephesians 2:4-6, what is your destiny?

4. What do the following verses say about Christ and/or me?
   - 2 Corinthians 5:21
   - Romans 4:5-8
   - Romans 5:1-2
   - Romans 5:8-9

5. What are the fruits of the Spirit mentioned in Gal. 5:22? How does our justification (being declared right before God) help us love others the way God

intended? (Hint: think about the metaphor of the spiritual bank account).

For additional study:

Conduct a short survey of the phrase "royal robes" in Scripture. Consider what the robes signify in each passage.

- Gen. 41:42
- 1 Kings 10:24-26
- 2 Kings 22:8-20
- Isaiah 61:10
- Job 29:14
- Esther 5:1
- Ps. 132:9
- Zechariah 3:4
- Mark 12:38
- Acts 12:21
- Rev. 7:9-17
- Rev. 19:8
- Rev. 22:14

CHAPTER 4: DAUGHTERS OF THE KING

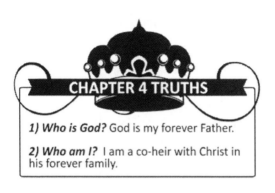

CHAPTER 4 TRUTHS

1) Who is God? God is my forever Father.

2) Who am I? I am a co-heir with Christ in his forever family.

There was once a woman who had it all together. She had everything she could ever imagine – a name and career, loving family, a lavish home, and more riches than she could ever spend. Everything seemed to be going her way.

But one day she messed up. She did something wrong – terribly wrong – and got caught. The woman was found guilty, sentenced by a judge, and sat in prison on death row awaiting her punishment. The shame of her mistake was only overshadowed by the knowledge of what she had lost – everything.

But just when it looked like the inevitable would take place, the unexpected happened. After years of sitting in a cold cement cell, the jailor told her she was scheduled for release. And not only that, but her record had been expunged. There would be no record of her crime or her sentencing, so no one could testify against her at a later date.

The woman walked out of the prison and stepped into the light, letting the sun warm her face for the first time in years. She couldn't help but smile knowing that her old way of life was now behind her. She had a chance. She had a new life to walk toward. She felt like the luckiest woman alive.

This woman's story would make for a pretty good movie if that were the end, but it's not. Because even though she had already experienced the unexpected, the unthinkable happened next. Outside the prison, someone was waiting for her. A man opened a car door and asked her to get inside. He said he was going to take her to her new home.

The woman, who was incredibly curious and also a good bit suspicious, asked the requisite questions and discovered it was this man who secured her release from prison. He worked at the bidding of his father, he said. And now, he explained, he wanted to take her to meet his father.

"Your father?" the woman wondered. "Who is your father?"

And the man just smiled and said, "My father is now your father. I have come to take you to him. He wants you to live with him, enjoy the food from his table. He wants to provide for you as his daughter – give you every single thing you need. In fact, he wants to give you everything he has."

At this, the woman was completely flabbergasted.

"But why?" she said. "Why would you and your father want to do all those things for me? I don't even know you. Besides, I am guilty! I really did that bad thing back there. Why would you want to rescue me when I truly deserved to die in that jail?"

The man said: "Because My father loves you."

This story isn't entirely fictional. I borrowed this metaphor from author Jerry Bridges and turned it into a story for us because this could very well be the story of any one of us.[12] In fact, if we have been declared right by God, this *is* our story. And this is how our story unfolds: after God justifies us (declares us right), he adopts us.

In chapter 3, we discovered that God is our righteous Judge who judges our sin. But we also learned that it is through his righteousness (his faithfulness to his promises) that he pardons our sin as well. And he accomplishes our pardon without neglecting justice by redeeming us through Christ. He sends his perfect Son to die on the cross in our place, securing our release from the spiritual prison in which we all find ourselves – sin.

We are, just like the woman in the story, set free from sin. And not only that, but our records are expunged, wiped clean. Our sin is transferred to Christ, and we get Christ's perfect record. We are able to walk away from death and its dark prison as free women. But in this chapter, we're going to discover that God doesn't stop there. He doesn't just do the unexpected, he does the unthinkable. After he justifies us, he adopts us. Our Creator, Savior, and Judge becomes our forever Father.

WHO IS GOD? GOD IS MY FOREVER FATHER

In the previous chapter, we read from the book of Galatians, a book Paul wrote to new and young believers in the churches of Galatia (modern-day Turkey). He wrote to them to remind them that they had been set free from living under the curse of the Law (Gal. 3:10; see also Rom. 7:7-12). In Christ, God set them free from having to strive to meet God's standard of holiness, and gave them a new, clean record and then adopted them as sons and daughters.

Gal. 4:4-7 says, "But when the set time had fully come, God sent his Son, born of a woman, born under the law, [5] to redeem those under the law, that we might receive adoption to sonship. 6 Because you are his sons, God sent the Spirit of his Son into our hearts, the Spirit who calls out, 'Abba, Father.' 7 So you are no longer a slave, but God's child; and since you are his child, God has made you also an heir" (NIV).

I want you to note a couple of things here. First, after we are justified (declared right), we are set free from sin. But God doesn't stop there. He doesn't just "redeem" us or buy us out of slavery and then set us free to go along our merry way saying, *"Good luck out there in the real world!"* Rather, God adopts us into his eternal family. At its heart, this is what it means to be a Christian. We have, through Christ, been brought into God's eternal family. And when God adopts us, he becomes our forever Father.

When Scripture calls God our Father, it isn't just using a metaphor to describe God, such as he is the Rock, or Door, or even a nursing mother (Deut. 32:4; John 10:9-16; Num. 11:12). God is not just *like* a father, he *is* a Father.[13]

Through faith, Paul says in Gal. 4:6, God becomes our Abba Father. That term 'Abba' is a personal, intimate term. If you had to translate it into English, the closest you could come is "daddy." It is a very tender title. Most importantly, Abba is a word that Jesus himself used to describe his relationship with God (Mark 14:36).

And now, by faith, you and I get to enter into that relationship. Paul says, here in Galatians, that God also becomes our "Abba" Father. The God who is our Creator (chapter 1), the God who is our Savior (chapter 2), and the God who is our Righteous Judge/Justifier (chapter 3) is now our tender and loving Father. That means first and foremost that we belong to him.

After working with a few Muslim students in our community, I became very interested in learning about their culture. A friend of mine who serves as missionary to Muslim communities suggested I read the book, *Princess: A*

True Story of Life Behind the Veil in Saudi Arabia, the biography of a Saudi princess named Sultana who, despite having a privileged position and being related to the King of her nation, lived a tragic life merely due to her gender.

Despite the blue blood coursing through her veins, her father rarely addressed her. In fact, she wasn't allowed to speak to him unless he spoke first. Her requests and concerns were always ignored unless they were channeled through a male spokesman. And because she was expected to remain in her room or living quarters having no other contact except with family and household staff, the princess battled loneliness and depression. She bore her father's name, but it was a barren title.

Unlike Sultana's father, having the Creator of the universe as our Father brings with it certain rights and privileges. When our heavenly Father adopts us into his family, we have special access to him and his throne. We get to talk to him in prayer and through his Holy Spirit. We are privileged to learn from him, receiving wisdom and guidance each and every time we ask. We enjoy spending time with him, in his very presence.

But in reading the biography of Sultana, I was struck by the difference between our world's understanding of royalty and position and how such realities are framed in Scripture. In some parts of the world, fathers are viewed as the supreme authority based on their gender alone. But in our culture, we often dismiss fatherhood as largely irrelevant.

Of all parts of the globe, the west has perhaps the poorest view of fathers in general. I was scrolling through Facebook recently and came across a chart posted by a friend. The chart had two columns and on the left column were listed 10 things kids ask their mother on a daily basis. Common questions like: "When are we?" "Where are we" and "Why aren't we?"

The left column designated all the things kids ask their fathers, but it only had one question: "Where's Mom?" This list easily sums up our culture's view of fathers: we view them as unnecessary.

Also very common in our culture is the underlying perception that by virtue of their gender, fathers are somehow genetically inferior – intellectually, emotionally – to women.

For instance, they need diagrams for completing basic caregiving activities like dressing their children. Another little gem I found on Facebook showed a photo of a white onesie with big red letters printed on the front. It read, "You can do this, Dad!" And it had arrows printed toward the arm holes where "arms" was printed. Another set of arrows and the word "legs" pointed to the openings at the bottom.

For a variety of reasons, fatherhood has become characterized in our culture by the deadbeat dad, who, because of either a midlife crisis or extended adolescence, is clueless or prone to idiocy. Worse still, our culture practically expects fathers to disengage from their families emotionally, physically, and financially. So, instead of garnering a place of honor, fathers in our culture have become objects of ridicule.

Because of the two extremes, women around the world often have trouble relating or understanding God as a Father. Our experiences with less-than-honorable earthly fathers taint how we relate to our heavenly Father. If our earthly father was harsh, we believe God must be unrelenting or impossible to deal with, too. If our earthly father was distant and cold, we surmise God to be the same.

So, I want to be as plain as I can when I say this. No. No. No. No. No. No!

Sadly, both of these worlds miss out on God's glorious purpose for the Father-child relationship. God, as our forever Father, is a loving Father. He is the sum total and more than what our earthly fathers should be and could be.

THE LOVE OF OUR FOREVER FATHER:

His love is **great** (Eph. 2:4)
His love **surpasses knowledge** (Eph. 3:19)
His love is full of **goodness** (Ps. 69:16)
His love is **lavish** (1 John 3:1)
His love binds us with **kindness** (Hosea 11:4)
His love is **wonderful** (Ps. 31:21)
His love is **priceless** (Ps. 36:7)
His love **never fails** (Ps. 36:7)
His love is **sacrificial** (1 John 4:9-10)
His love is **holy** (Ps. 103:1-4)
His love stands **firm** (Ps. 89:2)
His love is **unbreakable** (Rom. 8:38-39)
His love is **protective** (Lam. 3:22-23)
His love is **personal** (Ps. 121:3-8)
His love is **eternal** (Ps. 72:5)

Consider some of the ways God loves us from the chart in this chapter. The verses listed underscore one determinative reality: our adoption into God's family offers us a security and stability that some of us in this life have not ever known with our earthly fathers.

When you are adopted into God's family and become his daughter, he loves you with an eternal, unchanging love. God's love for you is not based on what you do or what you don't do, or even what's been done *to* you. How can you be sure that God is an honorable, loving Father? Because our forever Father loves us the way he loves his Son. Think about the relationship God the Father has with God the Son. The way God loves Jesus is the way he loves YOU! For many of us, like that woman in our story, that is not only unexpected, it is unthinkable, but it's true.

Listen to Jesus' words in John 17:24-26. In this passage, Christ is praying to God before he is arrested and crucified on the cross. He is addressing God as Father, and I want you to note here that Christ is praying not for himself – for the gruesome task ahead - but for his disciples and ultimately the world.

In verse 24 Jesus says, "²⁴ Father, I desire that they also, whom you have given me, may be with me where I am, to see my glory that you have given me because you loved me before the foundation of the world."

So, God loved Jesus before the foundation of the world. They have an eternal relationship characterized by love. And this is what Jesus wants the disciples to see and know and experience – the love between the Father and the Son.

Then in verses 25-26 he says, "O righteous Father, even though the world does not know you, I know you, and these know that you have sent me. ²⁶ I made known to them your name, and I will continue to make it known, that the love with which you have loved me may be in them, and I in them."

The relationship shared by the Father and Son is personal, intimate. This is why Jesus came. Not *simply* to justify us and declare us right. Not *simply* to free us from sin, but to bring us into his eternal family. Like in our story, Jesus secured that woman's release from prison, but then he took her back to his Father's house to meet and live with his forever Father. If you could characterize a purpose for Jesus's mission on earth, this was it: to introduce us to his Father.

How can you know that God is an honorable, loving Father? Because our forever Father loves us the way he loves his Son. Adoption is not just a bonus of our salvation. It isn't just the cherry on top of the proverbial salvation sundae – a great result or benefit of being redeemed.

Adoption is where God has been moving us this whole time. God in Christ saved us *from* sin *for* something. We have been saved *from* sin *to* Someone. We have gone from being "children of wrath," Paul tells us in Eph. 2:1, to becoming God's children. This was God's plan from the very beginning, before he ever created the universe.

Our adoption into God's family was no after-thought. Nor is it a mere side-benefit of our salvation. Our adoption is everything. Adoption is at its very heart what Christianity is all about. Christianity is not just one religious system among a plethora of other choices. It is about becoming related to a forever Father, and no other religion dares to make the same claim.

WHO AM I? I AM A CO-HEIR WITH CHRIST

So, when God adopts us into his forever family and becomes our forever Father, we get to have an intimate relationship with him. We share his home with him. We dwell with him in peace, and this new home blows the Garden of Eden out of the water! We are also called by his name. God's name reveals his holy character, and when he shares his name with us, we share in his holiness. But a new home and a new name are not the only privileges we enjoy as daughters of the King. Something else changes when we are adopted.

When we are adopted, we are given a new standing – a new position – before him. We become a co-heir with Christ. Go back to John 17:26, the end of Jesus' prayer. Jesus says, "I made known to them your name, and I will continue to make it known, that the love with which you have loved me may be in them, and I in them" (emphasis mine).

Here's what Jesus means. When we are adopted, we are united in Christ in a special way and that impacts the way we relate to God.

In the previous chapter, we discovered our justification (being declared right) means our destiny becomes Christ's destiny. What happened to Christ will happen to us. We will be raised together with him, and we will be seated together with him in the heavenly places (Eph. 2:4-6).

When we are adopted, we are united with Christ and that changes our standing before God. We become like Christ, a co-heir of everything our Father owns. So, who am I? Because I am adopted by God, I am a co-heir with Christ.

My sister and brother-in-law, along with their daughter, Gwen (6), recently adopted two small children through foster care, Noelle (4) and Titus (2). They are a sibling set, and based on their past family relationship the only things they stood to inherit were poverty, pain, hardship, trauma, and more. And after a lengthy legal proceeding, my sister and her husband put those precious children in their car and drove them to their new home. They shared with their new children the food from their table, their life and worldview, all their love, and one day they will give everything they own to all their children. Nothing will be held back.

When we are adopted into God's forever family, we become not just God's children, not just recipients of his never ending, never failing love, but we stand to inherit what God owns. Along with his other Son, we become an heir.

So, what do we get? What is our inheritance? As part of God's family, we inherit many things – but there are two main parts to our inheritance that I want to unpack.

As a co-heir with Christ, we inherit eternal life

The preschoolers at our church recently memorized John 3:16: "For God so loved the world that he gave his only begotten Son, that whosoever believes in Him, shall not perish but have everlasting life."

When I was a child that was one of the first Bible verses I memorized. It's an important one because it introduces even the smallest soul to the truth that God's love for them was so big it sent Christ to die so that they can have eternal life.

But somewhere in my childhood, I came to categorize 'eternal life' as something it isn't. I thought eternal life just meant I get to go to heaven and live a really, really long time. Eternal life became about a place and a thing. It became about getting to go to heaven. It became about living forever.

But that's not how Jesus explained eternal life. Look at John 17:3 in that same prayer Jesus prayed before his death: "3And this is eternal life, that they know you the only true God, and Jesus Christ whom you have sent."

Eternal life is *knowing* God, *knowing* his Son. Eternal life is being a part of–in a real, intimate, personal way–God's forever family. Eternal life is not entirely about a place or a thing, it's about a Person. It's about living with our forever Father all because of his Son. And yes, that happens in heaven, but it starts here, right now. We receive part of that inheritance now as we learn what it means to live *with* and *know* our heavenly Father in the dawn of his kingdom (Matt. 19:16-30).

I can start my new life by dwelling and abiding with Christ in his kingdom today because he has put his Spirit in me (Gal. 4:6). God's Spirit in us testifies that we are part of God's Family. God's Spirit in us acts as a down payment of our inheritance yet to come. As a co-heir with Christ, I stand to inherit eternal life; I stand to inherit the Father himself! There is no greater reward than to be forever united with him who is Life, Peace, and our Rest. All that starts now. We can enter into his kingdom to fulfill our calling as his servant kings today, knowing that an even greater inheritance is yet to come.

As a co-heir with Christ, we inherit a family business

But there is another aspect to the inheritance we receive

when we enter into God's forever family. Not only do we stand to inherit eternal life (our Father), but we also stand to inherit his family business. Jesus, as our brother, runs the business. God has declared him CEO of these family activities. What are those activities?

In John 17:4, 20-23 Jesus says, "4 I have brought you glory on earth by finishing the work you gave me to do...20My prayer is not for them alone. I pray also for those who will believe in me through their message, 21 that all of them may be one, Father, just as you are in me and I am in you. May they also be in us so that the world may believe that you have sent me. 22 I have given them the glory that you gave me, that they may be one as we are one– 23 I in them and you in me–so that they may be brought to complete unity" (emphasis mine).

Jesus' work was to bring others into his forever family. And before Christ ascended to heaven, he handed over this family business to us – the remaining members of his family still hanging around on the earth. Being called by God's name doesn't just mean we get a stellar reputation or a posh seat on a throne, it means we have real work to do.

Our job, then, is to draw others into this family (Matt. 28:16-20). Our job is to direct people to the Father through the Son, who is our brother! That is what Christ did when he was on earth. He brought people to his Father. This is part of what it means to have an eternal inheritance, bringing others into our forever family so that they, too, can enjoy this communion between the Father, the Son, and the Holy Spirit.

Our adoption, then, is not just about us – the security we get from being part of God's family, the sense of belonging we feel, the inheritance we stand to gain in the end (even our eternal life!). Our adoption is about our forever Father. Our adoption is about inheriting the Father's family business. We are finally able to live the life of rest we were intended to live from the very beginning so that others might see it and want to be added to our eternal family.

CHAPTER 4 TAKEAWAYS

When God adopts me, I get a forever family

When God adopts me, I get a forever family. And that family is eternal just like our Father is.

So, the person who sits next to you at the office or in class, she's your sister or brother if you've both been adopted by God. They aren't simply your co-worker or peer, someone you like or dislike – they are part of your family in Christ. Yep, you're going to be spending a lot of time with her! Right now, even though you might not think that's a good thing, our adoption into the family of God should impact how we treat our sisters and brothers in Christ.

Think about how we treat others in our homes. Sometimes the people in our homes can be the very hardest to love the way Christ loves them. Moms, for those of us who have children in our homes who already know Christ, we are obligated to treat them as brothers and sisters in the Lord. That should inform our words and tone, but it also should inform our instruction and expectations for righteousness.

Daughters, the way you speak and act or react to your parents should be informed by the fact that not only are they your parents and in a position of authority over you, but they are also your brothers and sisters in Christ and have been crowned by God as his son and daughter. They've been created for glory and called by his name. So, your words and interactions toward your parents should be mediated with honor and respect.

Wives, the same goes for how we treat our husbands

who are in Christ. They are to be treated as a brother redeemed by Christ and elevated to the same position of honor we find ourselves.

Even if our loved ones have yet to know Christ, the fact that they are God's good creation, bearing his image and created for his glory still obligates us to show respect. In the interim, we can pray that they will fully step into God's family and one day bear his name as well.

But not just in our homes, think about how we treat others in our church. If we are all redeemed by the exact same Christ, with the same exact amount of his blood, if we are all brought to live in the same house, clothed in the same royal robes, then no one is better than the other. We are all equal.

So, thoughts like *"I'm better than her, because I'm the first to sign up for stuff,"* or *"She's really got problems because I don't have that specific struggle"* are totally off-base. When we circulate those thoughts in our hearts and heads, we are going back to our old bank account, that old way of life, and living under the curse of the Law.

But the opposite can be true too. We can have a reverse form of pride and elevate others to high positions that don't even exist in God's family. It's easy to think things like: *"I wish I was as spiritual as she was. I'll never know as much as her,"* or *"I'll never have it as together as she does. Woe is me. Nobody likes me. I think I'll go eat worms."*

We can joke about some of those thoughts (ok, maybe not the worms part), but sometimes we really have them! I'm making a plea right now as daughters of the King and sisters in Christ: we gotta get over ourselves! Once adopted, our lives are about the forever Father who shares his title and glory with all members of his family equally and liberally. Each of us equally bears his name. Each of us equally showcases his glory. Each of us equally shares in the same inheritance.

When God adopts me, I have great hope

When we are adopted, God gives us a lavish home to which we are unaccustomed, an unbreakable family, a place of security and belonging, an unshakeable self-worth, a new name, a new purpose, ample provisions, and eternal blessings of love. We couldn't come up with a better set-up if we married a real-life prince, who we also discovered manufactured eternal youth pills.

But there is a greater reality to come. We stand to gain an even greater inheritance as God's daughters that will bring us an even greater hope. In previous chapters we learned that our justification results in sharing Christ's destiny. So, what is Christ's destiny? Christ stands to inherit the world - the new heavens and new earth that God is presently making (Is. 65:17). And because we are now united with Christ in this forever family, we share in Christ's glory. We are an heir of this kingdom along with Christ.

Our spiritual adoption means we have a greater hope than we could possibly imagine. We can face difficulties and suffering knowing that our forever Father is with us in the present and waiting for us in the future. Things won't always be the way they are now. This is our final hope: one day Christ will make all things right. One day there will be no dry bank accounts, no empty tables, no barren wombs, no final or sudden goodbyes (Rev. 21). Hungry mouths, broken hearts, and dark corners of the world will be wiped from our memory (Is. 61). It is to this hope that we can confidently cling.

As daughters of the Most High King and confidants of our loving eternal Father, we have an imperishable inheritance waiting for us. And in the meantime, he has surrounded us here on the earth with his extended family to love us, encourage us, challenge us, and equip us to invite more to his table and into his home.

It is unexpected. It is unthinkable. But it's true. We are crowned by our King, created for glory and called by his name, now it's our job to call others to do and be the same.

1. What kind of Father is God according to Ps. 103:13-18?

2. Has your relationship with your earthly father impacted your view of God as your Heavenly Father? How so?

3. What truth from chapter 3 spoke to your heart the most?

4. When we are adopted by God, we receive eternal life. What is eternal life according to John 17:3?

5. Write down the names of three family members, friends, or co-workers who do not know God as Father. Pray for an opportunity to share with them about the love your heavenly Father has shown you.

For additional study:

Consider a problem you're currently battling. How does being a child of God and having a forever Father in a forever family impact the way you respond? (Hint: Look up 1 Peter 1:4-6 and see what it says about the nature of our inheritance in Christ).

CHAPTER 5: HEIRS OF GRACE

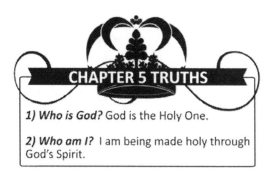

CHAPTER 5 TRUTHS

1) Who is God? God is the Holy One.

2) Who am I? I am being made holy through God's Spirit.

After a museum visitor fell and tore one of Pablo Picasso's masterpieces, it was painstakingly restored and returned to its place on the gallery wall. Concerning the restoration process, the *New York Times* reported, "To the untutored eye little is different about 'The Actor,' the Metropolitan Museum of Art's rare Rose Period Picasso, other than that it is now safely behind Plexiglas. It's virtually impossible to tell that on a January afternoon a woman taking an adult education class accidentally fell into the canvas, causing a six-inch vertical tear along the lower right-hand corner."[14]

"It was tedious," the restorer said. "But there's only one of these paintings, so the effort was worth it." Something priceless was broken. Throwing it away wasn't an option because there was only one. It had to be restored.

My goal for this book is to help women uncover foundational truths about their personal identity as one crowned and commissioned by the King of the world. In chapter 1, we learned we are God's good creation, made in his very image to be a masterpiece reflecting his artistry. We discovered that the image we bear pertains to both *who* we are and *what* we do.

In chapter 2, we discovered that sin corrupted that image in us. And although we still bear it, we don't mirror God's goodness perfectly. As a result, we lose what it means to be truly human – created for his glory and called by his name.

In chapters 3 and 4, we discovered that God provides a way to cover our sin, healing his image within. He sent his Son to live the perfect life, showing us what the true image of God looks like as it's lived out on earth, and then sent him to die our death on the cross. Because of the work of Christ, we are able to enter into the presence of God and become his daughters once again.

And in this final chapter, we will uncover how God's image within us is restored. We'll uncover how it is that we can go from being less than human–less than what God intended when he created us–to becoming fully human again. In chapter 5, we come full circle; we learn *how* our crowns are restored to us. And as any museum restorer will attest, the restoration process doesn't happen overnight. It's why we still struggle with sin. It's why we still have desires to return to those old ways of life and try to make withdrawals from that old bank account.

Being restored is a process.

WHO IS GOD? GOD IS THE HOLY ONE WHO SANCTIFIES ME

Our lengthy restoration process starts with a God who

is holy. Scripture tells us everything about God is holy - his name, his character, and his activity (Ps. 99:3-9). Because he is holy, he exists in a holy realm and anything that pertains to him and enters into the realm of his holiness, must also be holy.

In the Old Testament, when something or someone is called holy, that person or thing is set apart for God to serve him. That person or thing is sanctified or consecrated as special. In his opening words to the church at Corinth, Paul says believers are holy, not because we do everything right, but because we have been set apart for God.

First Cor. 1:2 says, "To the church of God in Corinth, to those <u>sanctified</u> in Christ Jesus and <u>called to be his holy people</u>..." (NIV, emphasis mine). Paul means that those of us who have been justified (declared right) are called God's holy people. The NKJV says, "...called to be saints..." And in order for us to become "holy people" or "saints," we first must be "set apart."

This process of being set apart for God in holiness is called *sanctification*. At its heart, to sanctify means to separate or set apart. It means to set apart what is holy from what is unholy. In sanctification, *God claims us as his and cleanses us from sin to make us holy like him*. Each of the King's daughters enters into this process of being sanctified, set apart from sin to him. This is what it means to walk in true humanity, to become what God intended for Adam and Eve. When God sanctifies us, we enter into the process of becoming like him – holy.

TO SANCTIFY: God *claims* us as his and *cleanses* us from sin to make us holy like him.

God claims me as his through his Spirit

So, what does this process of becoming sanctified entail?

First Pet. 2:9 tells us. The letters of 1 & 2 Peter were written by Peter just prior to the reign of the Roman Emperor Nero who violently and vehemently persecuted Christians (64 A.D.). Peter wrote these two letters to encourage believers in Christ-like living despite the dangerous times in which they found themselves. His words still ring for many believers experiencing similar suffering at the hands of brutal governments and secular cultures.

Listen to Peter's admonition in verse 9: "9But you are a chosen people, a royal priesthood, a holy nation, God's special possession, that you may declare the praises of him who called you out of darkness into his wonderful light."

Through Christ we have been set apart for God. God claims us. We are his "special possession." This is often called *positional sanctification* because in and through Christ our position has changed. Our old position was sinner; our new position is saint. We are a part of a holy group of people, and we belong to Christ.

In chapter 4, we learned that as a result of our adoption into God's forever family, God's daughters receive a special inheritance. And that inheritance includes several things – eternal life (which we said wasn't just living a really, really long time in heaven, but life with the Father in his kingdom) and a share in the Father's family business. The blessings of our divine inheritance are indeed amazing.

But when we are sanctified, we become Christ's inheritance. We are set apart by his Spirit for HIM! And proof of that fact is the Spirit who dwells in us. At conversion, God gives us his Spirit to testify that we belong to him (Gal. 4:4-6). It is this Spirit that cries out "Abba Father," proving that we have been adopted by him.

The Spirit testifies that God has claimed us and sanctified us – set us apart to himself as his inheritance. In adoption, we make much of what *we* stand to gain in the end. In sanctification, God makes much of what *he* gains in the end – a holy people. In sanctification, God claims me as his through his Spirit.

God cleanses me from sin through his Spirit

It took Lucy Belloli, a conservator at the New York Metropolitan Museum of Art, three months to repair the Pablo Picasso painting. She told the *New York Times* after the restoration was complete that the conservators had to act quickly because canvases, like people, "have a memory." The article said, "...the torn portion of the canvas had to be gently coaxed back to its flat state, otherwise it would have a tendency to return to the distortion left by the accident."[15]

Restoration involved a slow and careful realignment of the painting, and that meant time. For six weeks "The Actor" lay face down, with varying weights on it to counteract the "memory" of the damage.

First, Ms. Belloli said, she placed small silk sand bags that she made herself on the affected area; then slightly heavier ones, the kind seamstresses use to hold a pattern in place, and gradually heavier and heavier weights, stopping at one pound. Once the canvas seemed stabilized, she placed a Mylar patch on the back.

There is another element to our sanctification besides being claimed by God (positional sanctification). In this restoration process of sanctification, we aren't just *claimed* by God, we are also *cleansed* by him. We are brought back into alignment to our original place and position with him.

Romans 8:1-4 says, "Therefore, there is now no condemnation for those who are in Christ Jesus, [2] because through Christ Jesus the law of the Spirit who gives life has set you free from the law of sin and death. [3] For what the law was powerless to do because it was weakened by the flesh, God did by sending his own Son in the likeness of sinful flesh to be a sin offering. And so he condemned sin in the flesh, [4] in order that the righteous requirement of the law might be fully met in us, who do not live according to the flesh but according to the Spirit."

Before we were justified in Christ, we lived a cursed life trying to keep all the rules. We lived in sin. But as our Savior, God allowed for a great exchange. And now, we are justified (declared right) by God through Christ, as if we had kept the whole law. It's as if we have exchanged bank accounts with Christ. And now we see before us a new bank account labeled Spirit instead of the old debt-ridden bank account labeled flesh. But despite our new resources, we each possess the tendency to return to the distortion of sin. Paul warns us against such a temptation in Rom. 8: 5-17.

"Those who live according to the flesh have their minds set on what the flesh desires; but those who live in accordance with the Spirit have their minds set on what the Spirit desires. 6 The mind governed by the flesh is death, but the mind governed by the Spirit is life and peace. 7 The mind governed by the flesh is hostile to God; it does not submit to God's law, nor can it do so. 8 Those who are in the realm of the flesh cannot please God. 9 You, however, are not in the realm of the flesh but are in the realm of the Spirit, if indeed the Spirit of God lives in you. And if anyone does not have the Spirit of Christ, they do not belong to Christ. 10 But if Christ is in you, then even though your body is subject to death because of sin, the Spirit gives life because of righteousness. 11 And if the Spirit of him who raised Jesus from the dead is living in you, he who raised Christ from the dead will also give life to your mortal bodies because of his Spirit who lives in you.

12 Therefore, brothers and sisters, we have an obligation—but it is not to the flesh, to live according to it. 13 For if you live according to the flesh, you will die; but if by the Spirit you put to death the misdeeds of the body, you will live.

14 For those who are led by the Spirit of God are the children of God. 15 The Spirit you received does not make you slaves, so that you live in fear again; rather, the Spirit you received brought about your adoption to sonship. And by him we cry, 'Abba, Father.'[16] The Spirit himself testifies with our spirit that we are God's children. [17] Now if we are children, then we are heirs—heirs of God and co-heirs with Christ, if indeed we share in his sufferings in order that we may also share in his glory."

The work of the Spirit in our hearts not only *claims* that we belong to God, but the Spirit also *cleanses* us from within so that our desires increasingly align with God's. The Spirit's continual, gradual work in our lives puts to death "the misdeeds of the body" as Paul says in vs. 13. Internally, this looks like a heart transformation. Where our old heart desired things of the flesh, our new Spirit-filled heart longs after things of the spirit.

This is called *progressive sanctification.* We are, by the Spirit of God, changed day by day, bit by bit, increasingly set apart in who we are and what we do and what we think and what we feel. We are progressively cleansed and made holy; we begin to look more like God. Sanctification, then, is learning to live as Christ lived, not just inhaling and exhaling, but walking in and through his Spirit, as Paul says in vs. 13.

Sometimes this process of being changed into Christ's image can be painful. Imagine the weights used to counteract damage to a canvas in an art restoration project. While serving an important role in bringing the painting to its former glory, the weights become increasingly heavier depending on the size or depth of the tear in the masterpiece. Under their weight, the broken canvas is progressively reshaped. Progressive sanctification promises us that things will not always be as they are now. It also gives us confidence that the troubles and disappointments we experience even after we come to Christ are not without meaning and purpose.

Troubles are not, as some would suggest, indications of our unworthiness to serve, but rather indicators of the worthiness and wisdom of the One who is shaping us to look like him once again. Therefore, we can look at hardships and failures and know that there is a Master Artist working feverishly behind the scenes to complete his massive restoration project at just the right moment.

The crown of Christ does not promise an easy, strife-free life. Until God chooses the right time to restore the entire world, our lives and homes will continue to know trouble and sickness and disappointment. Our crowns ensure, however, that we can grab hold of peace and rest because we have access to the throne room of the King. In progressive sanctification, we can trust and hope and rest in Christ who gives us his Spirit as he completes our restoration to his image.

WHAT'S THE DIFFERENCE?
In **positional sanctification**, I contribute nothing. It's the Spirit's work.
In **progressive sanctification**, I contribute greatly. I must cooperate with the Spirit.

So, what is the difference between positional and progressive sanctification? In positional sanctification, *we contribute nothing*. It is wholly the Spirit's work in us that testifies we belong to Christ. It is his work to claim us, and make us his - individuals set apart for God.

However, in progressive sanctification, *we contribute greatly*. While we rely on the Spirit to guide, instruct, and empower us often through the weight of troubles, we are expected to cooperate, responding to trouble and trials with hope and trust. And to the degree that we choose to listen and obey the Spirit's promptings, we are made increasingly holy. It's why Paul says in Rom. 8:12, "Therefore, brothers and sisters, we have an obligation—but it is not to the flesh, to live according to it. [13] For if you live according to the flesh, you will die; but if by the Spirit you put to death the misdeeds of the body, you will live."

According to Paul, you contribute to the act of putting to death the misdeeds of the body. It matters the way you live. It's what keeps us from going on a sin-spree after we've been declared right by the cross. But putting to death the misdeeds of the body isn't always easy. Choosing to live in the Spirit is a true spiritual battle as we war against the desires of our flesh. And the only way we win this battle to be made holy is to ensure we're fighting on the right battlefield.

Imagine a general sending his soldiers to attack an enemy only to discover the enemy is not there. When the army arrives, they see evidence of them – cold fires, barracks, trash and litter – but the ambush only works if the enemy is present, if they've picked the right battlefield.

So often we look at our lives and problems and think, *"I really need to stop gossiping"* or *"I need to respond better to my kids,"* or *"I need to find better influences in my life,"* and we attack the problem on the wrong battlefront. We start by addressing behaviors rather than going to the root problem. This battle to be made holy, Paul says, doesn't just start with our hands, feet, or mouths. If we're going to stop overspending, hanging out with the wrong crowd, holding our tongues, then we have to wage war at the root of those issues. When God, through his Spirit, changes us, where does he start? He starts with our hearts and minds!

Rom. 8:5-7 says, "[5] Those who live according to the flesh have their *minds* set on what the flesh desires; but those who live in accordance with the Spirit have their *minds* set on what the Spirit desires. [6] The *mind* governed by the flesh is death, but the *mind* governed by the Spirit is life and peace" (emphasis mine).

This is where we have to contribute! We have to actively

set our minds on things of the Spirit. Because it is our minds (or hearts in the broad sense) that direct our feet, hands, and mouths, and everything else! Our minds and hearts are the real battlefields of sanctification.

That's why I've encouraged you to memorize Scripture to complement what you're learning in this book. It's not simply something we *should* do. Memorizing God's Word isn't simply a good idea. Meditating on the Scriptures is one way you can contribute to the sanctification process. We can't just simply stop thinking old thoughts – thoughts riddled with depression, anxiety, fear, anger, resentment. To see change in our lives, we must replace those old thoughts with new thoughts, with God's thoughts.

And when we do that, we are giving the Spirit something to work with as he changes us, as he makes us more holy. He is able to bring specific Scripture to our mind that we've embedded in our hearts at just the right moment - when we're battling old ways, old fears, old temptations. And as the Spirit brings victory in our minds, change comes to bear on our whole person – emotions, will, behaviors, and even our bodies.

Don't give up on your Scripture memory! It is one way God brings change to your life. It is one way he makes us more holy, more like him. And it is one way he increasingly sets us apart as his. In sanctification, God both claims and cleanses us through his Spirit. On one side, we contribute nothing. On the other, we contribute greatly.

WHO AM I? I AM BEING MADE HOLY BY GOD'S SPIRIT

Because I am claimed by God, I am set apart for his service

Being claimed by God, means that we are set apart for his service. We have already noted this, but in his opening words to the church at Corinth, Paul says in 1 Cor. 1:2 that we are *"sanctified in Christ Jesus"* and therefore, *"called to be his holy people..."* (NIV). The NKJV says, *"...called to be saints."* Because of our sanctification, we are called a saint! Depending on your church background, this may sound strange. But, simply speaking, Scripture defines a saint as someone who has been sanctified. Literally, the word "saint" means "holy ones."

I like how Jerry Bridges describes a saint in his book *Who Am I?* He writes, "Sainthood is not a spiritual attainment, or even a recognition of such attainment. It is rather a state or status into which God brings every believer. All Christians are saints. It is a very unfortunate and unhelpful thing that we so often misunderstand this short, simple word. To use a word that applies to all Christians in a way that suggests there is a special, elite class of Christians, is doubly wrong: it steals from the church important truths that God intended to communicate through the idea of sainthood, and it promotes jealousy and division within the body of Christ by suggesting a hierarchy that does not exist."[16]

So, when Paul calls us saints, he isn't saying we've suddenly become a super-Christian. God gives us crowns, not halos. Rather, our sainthood means we are finally able to fulfill that purpose for which God created us – for which God created Adam and Eve. We become holy, in that we are set apart by a holy God to serve him. Our crown is our commission.

In chapter 1, we learned that when God gave Adam his image, he tasked him with subduing the world, establishing him as his sub-regent or servant king. And as a servant of the throne, Adam was set apart to fulfill the Word of the Lord on earth. But sin messed everything up. Instead of being separated *to* God and dedicated *to* God, Adam became separated *from* God and dedicated only to himself. The result? The creation no longer reflected the artistry of its Maker. Adam became unholy, and us with him. But in Christ, through his Spirit, we are finally restored back to our grand purpose of being set apart to the Lord, set apart to serve him.

So, who am I? I am a saint being sanctified. And that means, in part, that I am *claimed* by a holy God and set apart to serve him in holiness.

Because I am being cleansed by God, I am being transformed into Christ's image

In cleansing me, God is transforming me into the image of his Son. Does that mean I won't ever sin? Even though we've been declared perfect, we will continue to sin. But God doesn't simply desire to *declare* us righteous, he wants to *make* us righteous, and that's why he enters into this slow and painstaking process to sanctify us.

Second Cor. 3:18 reveals what it looks like when we are fully restored:" "And we all, with unveiled face, <u>beholding the glory of the Lord</u>, are being transformed <u>into the same image</u> from one degree of glory to another. For this comes from the Lord who is the Spirit" (emphasis mine).

Paul tells us we are being transformed into an image of glory – and not just any image, but a specific image. Our sanctification means we are actively and progressively being transformed into the image of Christ. The Son, who is perfectly God, came and lived among us in a perfect way. On earth, Christ showed us what the image of God was intended to look like in humanity (2 Cor. 4:4 ; Col. 1:15). Christ was the perfect man and servant-King illustrating to all the world what life in the King's kingdom looked like.

In total, this picture of being made holy means God is at work to heal his image in each of us that became shattered in the Garden of Eden. Little by little, the image of God within us is being progressively renewed to look like Christ. We aren't just being made more holy or being made into a super-Christian. We are being made holy like Christ is holy.

In 1 Cor. 15:47-49, Paul gives a few more details about what we will look like, or rather *who* we will look like. In this passage, he discusses how our destiny becomes Christ's destiny, and he says, "The first man was of the dust of the earth; the second man is of heaven. [48] As was the earthly man, so are those who are of the earth; and as is the heavenly man, so also are those who are of heaven. [49] <u>And just as we have borne the image of the earthly man, so shall we bear the image of the heavenly man</u>" (emphasis mine).

Just like the image of God was passed down to us from Adam (broken, corrupted, in need of repair), if we are in Christ, if we are his, if we are claimed by him, then by the Spirit, that image within us is being progressively changed into the image of the second Adam – the heavenly man – Jesus Christ.

This is the core of our personal identity! It is not simply our personality or our biology. We are not to define ourselves solely by our likes or dislikes. Nor are we to define ourselves simply by the everyday roles we fill – mom, teacher, minister, doctor, chauffeur, culinary extraordinaire. Neither are we to define ourselves by our favorite activities or how well we perform them - how well we sing, write, dance, cook or craft.

We are to define ourselves, first and foremost, according to Christ. It is where God is moving us by his Spirit and with our help. Truly, we are created for glory, sharing God's image and being progressively restored to look like God's Son. The more we begin to view God properly, the clearer and more accurate understanding we get of ourselves – those of us who are being renewed inwardly to look like him.

So, who is God?

- God is my good Creator.
- God is my Savior.

- God is my righteous Judge.
- God is my forever Father.
- God is my holy King.

And what does God do?

- God created me for glory and crowned me with his image.
- He saved me from sin and rebellion against his throne.
- He redeemed me from living under death and in debt to the law and gave me the royal robes of righteousness worn by his Son.
- He adopted me into his forever family and gave me his name and the title Daughter of the King.
- He shared his glory with me making me a co-heir of his kingdom with Christ.
- He claimed me as his and is cleansing me so that I may be set apart for holy service in his kingdom.

That means, I am:

- A divine image-bearer
- Redeemed from sin
- A beloved daughter
- Spirit-filled sister to billions
- An heir of the kingdom
- And a saint of the most holy God.

We can trust that God is at work in our lives. The Master Artist designed us perfectly. We fall and do irreparable damage to ourselves, but the Artist – in Christ – transforms us into a masterpiece once again. Just as God created us in the very beginning, he will recreate us again.

And, because he is the sole agent in our restoration, we can trust him to finish the process. So, don't be discouraged if your transformation into Christ's image seems slow or at least slower than those around you. It is a process. And when Christ comes again, the Spirit will complete his work in our lives as our restoration is finally fulfilled. And we will look like him! We can trust that God's work in us will be more than a few patches here or there. God doesn't renovate us by keeping the faulty pieces of our lives intact. When God restores us, we are an entirely new creation – righteous and holy as Christ is (2 Cor. 5:17). Christ's kingdom destiny is and will fully become our kingdom destiny, too, glorifying God in all we say and do (1 Cor. 10:31). In Christ, we are and will be crowned - created for glory, called by his name.

1. Psalm 99:3-9 describes God as holy. In what ways is God holy in this passage?

2. According to 1 Peter 1:1-2, who sanctifies us? Is he the only person involved in this process? If not, who else participates, and how?

3. Getting a proper view of God gives us a proper view of ourselves. Which character trait/activity of God (listed below) has helped you better understand your personal identity and/or calling? Explain your answer.
   - God is my good Creator
   - God is my Savior
   - God is my righteous Judge
   - God is my forever Father
   - God is my holy King

4. In 1 John 3:1-3, we are told we won't always "look" as we do now. How will we be different?

For additional study:

According to 2 Cor. 4:4, Col. 1:15, and Heb. 1:3, Christ is the true image of God. Using a commentary or a site like BlueLetterBible.org, look up the Greek word for "image" used in these verses. (Tip: Blue Letter Bible provides a link to the Strong's number for "image" and an excerpt from Thayer's Greek Lexicon. Be sure to consult both resources).

Then consider the following: how does Christ as the "exact imprint" of God's nature impact the image of God within us? (1 Cor. 15:49)

ABOUT THE AUTHOR

MELISSA DEMING is the author of *Daughters of the King: Finding Your Place in the Biblical Story* and the creator of hiveresources.com - a site to help women sweeten their walk with Christ. She and her husband, Jonathan, have seven-year-old twins, Zacharias and Jonah. Melissa has a M.Div. in Women's Studies from Southeastern Baptist Theological Seminary, Wake Forest, N.C., and a B.A. in Journalism from Texas A&M University.

ABOUT THE ARTIST

ELLIE BENSON is an artist and designer and occasional writer living in Augusta, GA. She and her husband, Kenneth, and have two lovely daughters, Emma and Alice. Ellie and Kenneth's art and design business can be found at bensonbensonco.com. She writes on art, faith and family at ellieeugenia.com.

ENDNOTES

[1] http://www.csmonitor.com/USA/2010/0125/Visitor-tears-Picasso-s-The-Actor.-How-can-Met-fix-it

[2] http://www.csmonitor.com/USA/2010/0125/Visitor-tears-Picasso-s-The-Actor.-How-can-Met-fix-it

[3]
http://www.nytimes.com/2012/08/24/world/europe/botched-restoration-of-ecce-homo-fresco-shocks-spain.html?_r=0

[4] Thomas R. Schreiner, *The King in His Beauty: A Biblical Theology of the Old and New Testaments* (Grand Rapids: Baker Academic, 2013), 7.

[5] Hannah Anderson, *Made for More: An Invitation to Live in God's Image* (Chicago: Moody Publishers, 2014), 33.

[6] John Sailhamer, *The Expositor's Bible Commentary*: Vol. 2 (Grand Rapids: Zondervan, 1990), 45.

[7] Sailhamer, 51.

[8] Bruce Ware, *Big Truths for Young Hearts: Teaching and Learning the Greatness of God* (Wheaton: Crossway, 2009), 96.

[9] Visit my Daughters of the King Pinterest board to view pictures of these royal robes or visit this pin (https://www.pinterest.com/pin/57702438951997076/) directly.

[10] Visit
http://www.oremus.org/liturgy/coronation/cor1953b.html
for a full transcription of Her Majesty Queen Elizabeth II's

coronation on June 2, 1953.

11 Elyse Fitzpatrick, *Found in Him: The Joy of the Incarnation and Our Union with Christ* (Wheaton: Crossway, 2013), 193.

12 Jerry Bridges, *Who I Am? Identity in Christ* (Adelphi: Cruciform Press, 2012), 41.

13 Mary Kassian, *In My Father's House: Finding Your Heart's True Home* (Nashville: B&H Books, 2005), 314 in Kindle Reader.

14

http://www.nytimes.com/2010/04/21/arts/design/21pica sso.html?_r=0

15

http://www.nytimes.com/2010/04/21/arts/design/21pica sso.html

16 Bridges, 66.